THE CAREER CHANGE HANDBOOK

If you want to know how . . .

Passing Psychometric Tests
Know what to expect and get the job you want

Succeeding at Interviews
Give great answers and ask the right questions

Rob Yeung's Insider Guide to Successful Interviews
Proven tips to get you the job

Passing That Interview
Your step-by-step guide to coming out on top

Be Prepared!
Getting ready for job interviews

howtobooks

Please send for a free copy of the latest catalogue:

How To Books
Spring Hill House, Spring Hill Road
Begbroke, Oxford OX5 1RX
email: info@howtobooks.co.uk
http://www.howtobooks.co.uk

THE CAREER CHANGE HANDBOOK

REVISED AND UPDATED · THIRD EDITION · 3RD

HOW TO FIND OUT WHAT YOU'RE GOOD AT AND WHAT YOU ENJOY – THEN GET SOMEONE TO PAY YOU FOR IT.

GRAHAM GREEN

howto books

Published by How To Books Ltd,
Spring Hill House, Spring Hill Road,
Oxford OX5 1RX.
Tel: (01865) 375794. Fax: (01865) 379162
email: info@howtobooks.co.uk
http://www.howtobooks.co.uk

First published 2003
Second edition 2005
Third edition 2006

British Library Cataloguing in Publication Data
A catalogue record for this book is available from the British Library

ISBN 13: 978-1-84528-137-3
ISBN 10: 1-84528-137-3

Cover design by Baseline Arts Ltd, Oxford
Produced for How To Books by Deer Park Productions
Typeset by PDQ Typesetting, Newcastle-under-Lyme, Staffs.
Printed and bound in Great Britain

NOTE: The material contained in this book is set out in good faith for general
guidance and no liability can be accepted for loss or expense incurred as a result of
relying in particular circumstances on statements made in the book. The laws and
regulations are complex and liable to change, and readers should check the current
position with the relevant authorities before making personal arrangements.

Contents

Acknowledgements

I am indebted to many people who have helped and inspired me over the years. I have been particularly fortunate to have had many excellent bosses, who between them have taught me a great deal about managing and dealing with people in the world of work, however badly I may have handled things at the time. Most influential of all have been my European marketing colleagues in the Wiggins Teape Group during the period from 1965 to 1981, as intelligent, diverse and lively a bunch of individuals as one could possibly find anywhere.

Such expertise as I possess in career counselling and job search guidance has largely been acquired from my colleagues at Chusid Lander from 1990 to 1997. There seemed to be a spirit of some kind inhabiting the walls of the Fitzroy Street offices we occupied, which could perhaps be traced back to Frederick Chusid, who founded the business immediately after World War II in the USA. Certainly we cared about our clients. Most of all it is from my clients that I have learned; they invariably know best what they need and want when given the time and space to find it.

With respect to this book there are a few particular individuals to thank. First of all Lynn Hyatt, my colleague at Jo Ouston & Co, who pointed at my twenty pages of notes on Job Search Guidance, which I wrote back in the early nineties and said, 'You have a book there.' Nothing would have happened without that stimulus. Surprisingly quickly over the next few months it grew into this volume. Thanks too to Jo herself whose tacit support has been much appreciated.

Next in line come my two unofficial editors, Imogen McEvedy and Hashi Syedain – both genuine editors in real life – who very kindly read early and later drafts and suggested useful additional content. They managed to mix critical comments and enthusiastic support in just the right ratio, helping me greatly to improve the readability and 'sound' of the book – messy and incomprehensible bits remaining are the result of my own unaided effort. I am additionally indebted to Hashi for her research into the Internet, the source of most of

Appendix III – A guide to job-hunting on the Internet.

Finally I should like to thank my long-suffering wife, Shaune, who has encouraged and supported me through yet another consuming passion, consuming time that might otherwise have been available for more sociable activities or for gardening and other useful tasks.

'There is a secret to successful job search. It is persistence. Seek and you shall find.'

Graham Green

Preface to the third edition

Although change is nowadays said to be a permanent state that we all have to get used to, indeed to embrace, there really are a lot of things that do not change. It's a monstrous cliché but the most obvious unchanging thing is 'human nature'. Some would go further and claim that individual people do not change. However, we can and do change careers, though not I submit by changing ourselves. Unsurprisingly, to do this successfully you need the same four things you needed last year:

- real dissatisfaction with your current career or job (it is not enough to feel you ought to be doing something else);

- a *reasonable idea* of what you would prefer to be *doing*;

- a full understanding of the techniques you need to get from where you are to where you want to be (that's the job search bit); and

- the *determination* to get there.

Changing job or career is a human activity, and whatever we do we cannot escape the human interaction, and *that* doesn't change very much at all.

It seems to many of my clients that the employment situation, the world of work, is ranged against them, that they don't match up to what other people expect or want from them. The answer to the problem is always the same, and it lies within the client's own control.

You, the would-be job changer, need to know yourself, your capabilities and your potential, and you may also need a friend or a helper to enable you to clarify these matters for yourself. Then, having identified your strengths you can start to investigate where they can be enjoyably employed.

Good employers, in both the private and public sectors, have one question uppermost in their mind with respect to each candidate during the recruitment process: what can she or he do for our organisation? If you can't tell them you won't make the move you want to.

In one area things have changed a good deal. You've probably changed your computer since last year. If you are using Microsoft (I expect the same is true of Applemac users), you've been receiving almost daily 'updates' for your PC – they must change something I suppose. But strangely internet job search hasn't changed, except that you can get even more data even faster.

Some of the advances are quite sophisticated. I recently found one site, that of the Reed employment group, which showed how many applications had been received for each job advertised – useful. Mostly however it is 'more of the same', and I was pleased but slightly surprised to find that the best of the US career experts share my views about the internet (see Appendix III), except where they are even more negative!

To end this preface on a positive note, we still enjoy high employment in the UK, which means it must be a good time to change, so, good luck!

Graham Green

Introduction

Origins

This book has grown out of my practical experience as a career counsellor and out of various notes and guidelines I have written on different aspects of career counselling and job search. Firstly the book is for me. I have worked in career counselling and job search for over 15 years and have something to say about both. My apprenticeship was with the 'old school' of Chusid Lander, a career counselling company with its origins in the USA in the 1940s, which has been the major source of mainstream career counselling practice in the second half of the 20th century in the UK. One of the opening phrases at every seminar on job search conducted at Chusid Lander was '*The world of work is a world of people*'. It was meant to get across the message that people and how we deal with them are vital to success. Our main contribution was to help people to take a new look at themselves and supply them with the tools they needed to make their career move. That is also what this book is for, filtered through my eyes and personal experience.

I want to keep some of the best traditions alive and recognised as such, rather than dress them up and parade them as new. Genuine new technology is very useful and can and should be harnessed in the service of career counselling and job search, but its development has not changed anything important.

Audience

The book is written for people who are experiencing difficulty in their working life. They may be suffering from lack of self-belief, confusion of choice, absence of ideas or some other block or uncertainty which is preventing them from moving forward from a place they do not enjoy to one where they can satisfy most of their needs and some of their wants.

I have learned and continue to learn mostly from my clients – some thousand plus at the last rough count – who have kept me in touch with the world of work and have provided me with a continual supply of master classes in management. The book is therefore aimed at middle and senior management and professionals because they have been my clients.

I hope it will be of interest also to professional career counsellors who are not too proud to steal ideas. Most of mine are stolen, but I have stolen with as much discrimination as I could muster, though probably also on occasion without knowing it.

What it's about

The book is about the process of making a career move, not necessarily a career change, though that may also be involved. A necessary part of this is a job change whether it is within an organisation or out of one into another. Career moves may be major or minor and include straight-line progression or sideways moves to broaden experience. Whatever move you want to make it has to start from a basis of self-knowledge. In many cases this means that it forms part of some long-term strategy. Other people do not have strategic plans for their career; it is simply not the way they think about work.

Self-knowledge includes understanding your needs as well as your wants and, vitally, knowledge of what you can contribute to an organisation or an enterprise, for that is what you have to sell or capitalise upon – your skills, abilities, values, experience and knowledge.

Then you will need some degree of focus on what it is you want to do next. This can arrive as a direct result of increased self-knowledge, but mostly you need to set out deliberately to acquire it. Certainly the clearer and more comprehensive your focus, the more easily and directly other people will be able to help you. But even if you have no specific objective and a less than satisfactory (to you) degree of focus, you can and should proceed to the next phase. This is the preparation of your sales documentation, your main marketing tool, your CV.

Even without a clear objective you can produce a powerful CV, one which presents you and your key strengths clearly and positively. It starts with a pen portrait of you including a mix of attitudes, skills, abilities, background, and continues with career details emphasising your achievements and the contributions you have made in the course of your working life. Brief details of education and training, personal details and interests follow.

The world of work is a world of people, and if you talk, initially to those you know, then to others already doing what you could do and would enjoy doing, it will also help you find out where to get more and better information. This is how most people, whether they are aware of it or not, locate their next moves. This is 'networking', and when you acquire focus, which you can best achieve through networking, you will find that self-knowledge plus focus increases your self-confidence.

Philosophy

This book is really about people and, to some extent, about communication. The skill to communicate your key strengths to others plus the determination to keep going, especially when prospects seem bleak, will result in a successful move. It is a book based on an optimistic way of looking at the world. Organisations have aims and purposes that tend towards the public good. They fulfil needs or they wither. Some, of course, exploit their employees. This book might help indirectly to identify and avoid them.

I firmly believe that straightforwardness leads to better communication in all directions and that communication in a wider sense, requiring a longer book than this, is what living in the world is all about. I do not however believe in 'the whole truth'. There is no such thing outside the courts; indeed too much truth can confuse and even distort the **important** truths, important that is for job change, that need to be conveyed in CVs, letters, meetings and interviews.

Career change and development, and the process and techniques of job search make up a significant and important portion of our lives. We owe it to ourselves and to our families to find rewarding careers as part of a balanced life.

A successful career move involves people matching their ideas, passions and goals to the needs of employers and vice versa. People need jobs, and jobs need people.

The experience of others

The book can be read as a piece without interruptions for doing exercises, but there are exercises in the appendices to help you define your strengths and your aims. Throughout the book there are examples of letters and CVs that have worked well, worked well that is for the individuals who wrote them. **They are not models to be slavishly copied.** You must create your own approaches. There are also stories of successful clients who have achieved great things in their career development. I am grateful to be able to borrow from their success and of course I have chosen the best stories. You may not achieve their heights but if you follow their examples you will do well.

I have some opening advice. During your job search, whenever you find yourself in conversation with someone, remember these four things:

◆ **Listen. There is so much you can learn.**

◆ **Never be afraid to ask 'awkward' or 'daft' questions.**

◆ **Take opportunities to talk about your strengths in relation to your intended career move and work in general.**

◆ **Listen again. It is the greatest compliment you can pay another person.**

Finally remember the opening words of Dorothy Rowe's *Guide to Life* (Rowe 1995) 'The secret of life is that there is no secret.'

However, there is a secret to successful job search. It is **persistence**. Seek and you shall find.

There are just five ways of making a career move:

1. Get yourself known to an employer who is looking for someone like you.
2. Apply for an advertised job and get through the selection process.
3. Find (or more rarely be found by) a recruitment agent who has a suitable job.
4. Make an unsolicited approach to an organisation that needs your abilities, skills, etc.
5. Create your own business (not addressed in this book).

You can do it.

CHAPTER ONE

What Do You Really Want To Do?

This opening chapter shows you how to take a detailed, in-depth and all round look at yourself, how to discover your strengths through examining your experience and how to present these to others. It looks at the differences between people and points to exercises in the appendices. It shows you how to construct a 'label' for yourself that others will recognise and value. Finally it sets out how the job market functions and what you need to do to set about achieving a successful career move.

Do you know what you are looking for?

A surprisingly large number of people looking at the job market do not. They leaf through the job pages in the paper or surf the net, hoping to come across something that looks attractive. There is nothing wrong with doing this provided you are doing other things as well, but the chances of the magic job appearing before you are slight.

Once upon a time this didn't matter. In the public sector there was security with regular pay increments and a clear promotion route. Most companies in the private sector grew their own managers from regular intakes of trainees; it was common to find senior managers and board members with 20, 30 and 40 years' service behind them. At Bloggs United & Co many careers blossomed through the good offices of senior managers, who recognised their juniors' talents and moved them on.

It is not that things were necessarily better in the old days, and to a degree this kind of talent spotting and fostering still occurs, but it is getting rarer all the time. Many people do not know what career path to follow and drift through a series of jobs; they may be flexible and talented or just plain lucky, and have a good career, or they may miss out badly, never finding the right choices to make.

Why you need the right job

It is possible that some people will recognise the right job when they find it. Others just cannot work out what would be possible or best for them, so they stick to what they are doing provided it is not too irksome. It does not have to be that way. Serious problems can arise leading to severe stress or breakdown when people drift or get pushed into the wrong job and cannot find the way out. If you tolerate being in the wrong job not only will you suffer but your partner and your family will suffer too.

The secret is to know yourself, to know your key needs and wants and the difference between them, and to be able to find out how these can be met in a suitable and enjoyable career. Or, as the grandfather of one of my clients put it to him, 'Find out what you are good at and enjoy, and get someone to pay you for it!' It is as simple and as difficult as that.

Know and appreciate your strengths

People who know themselves well are those who over the years have had the benefit of perceptive feedback from others. Without this and without access to the value judgements that others make about us it is hard to get an accurate fix on our strengths and weaknesses; it is particularly difficult to evaluate properly our most obvious (to others) natural talents. Why for instance should someone place great value on an ability to create instant order out of a chaotic mess when for him/her

a) 'it is **so simple** just to arrange neat piles of items which go together' and

b) 'it is **so much easier** then to keep everything in order'?

How powerfully the truth of part (b) hits home to those of us who do not possess this ability. We find it little short of miraculous, because our experience after a serious attempt at part (a) is to find ourselves in more chaos of a different kind with items left over, which do not seem to belong anywhere in the new chaos!

We most of us tend to devalue what we find easy and forget that in certain contexts what we find easy and are good at is precisely what others want to know about us.

Employers in particular want to know what we are good at. They have a very good reason for wanting to know. They want to find out how much use we might be to their organisation. So to sell ourselves as effectively as possible we need to know ourselves and give proper weight to what we do well.

Who are you? What have you got to sell?

'**Who am I?**' This is one of those fundamental questions that philosophers have been asking themselves for centuries. Nevertheless it is one you need to make an attempt at answering if you want to enjoy your work. To set about this task you need to break things down a little. We all have:

Skills

These are things we have **learned** to do such as riding a bicycle, tying our shoelaces, operating the mouse on our computer. There are much more complicated ones too, which are more obviously career oriented, such as editing, or bookkeeping.

Attitudes or characteristics

These may be part of our make-up or derive from life experiences, e.g. optimism, pessimism, enthusiasm, determination, loyalty.

Values

There is no need to be coy about these. They may be the most important part of your make-up even if with time they may develop and change. Potential employers may or may not have mission statements. However, most organisations have a style or a reputation, which they are anxious to promote and in which they believe. Indeed they have values too, and it is important that they are consistent with your own.

Abilities

Abilities are natural talents we possess without having to learn them, they are things we are just good at. Doing jigsaw puzzles, dancing, or with reference to work, thinking logically, making a speech, persuading people to do things.

Experience

Experience includes past work of all kinds including achievements great and small. Appropriate analysis of achievements is the key to identifying **abilities.** (See also Appendix I.)

These are the things we can 'sell' to an employer, either naturally if we have the **ability** to sell, or when we have learned how to, if this is a **skill** we need to acquire. Let's look at them in turn:

Skills

As well as useful strengths in their own right skills can be indicators of abilities. The skill of watercolour painting could indicate an ability to observe. Only 'could' because a **skilfully executed** watercolour might have little resemblance to the subject and could therefore point to **inability** to observe. A recent client of mine claimed to be untalented and put any success down to 'just hard work – I have to work hard to learn and keep up with people who have real talents'. I put to him that he had 'an ability to work hard in all circumstances' which is not given to everybody. This is not only a genuine ability it is one of the best. I for one can only work hard under very restricted sets of conditions.

When you make your list of learned skills add some potential abilities that might go with them:

Skills	*Related abilities?*
Needlework	Ability to work with detail?
Dinner party food preparation	Creative presentation? Co-ordination?
Reading balance sheets	Analytical ability?

None of the above necessarily follow but they may in your case.

Attitudes or characteristics

We all have characteristics of which we are not proud, even perhaps ashamed. It is hard for many people to accept that it is permissible to be frightened of physical violence or to be shy and therefore hopeless at public speaking. These are ordinary human failings. Some we may be able with time and effort to do something about. We're concerned here with the more positive ones. These are real strengths, core bits of our personality that come through in a wide variety of circumstances. They characterise how we do things.

It is a fact that enthusiastic people do things enthusiastically (nine times out of ten at least). If you are such a person do remember that some people find this wearing on occasion.

They come in degrees of strength, as illustrated by the old irregular verbs:

- I am firm.
- You are stubborn.
- He/she is pig-headed.

Or
- I am tolerant.
- You are easygoing.
- He/she is lax.

If you class yourself as a pessimist, remember that there are undeniable virtues to be found in pessimism. Privately you may go through life never disappointed having always expected the worst. More positively with respect to the world of work your natural pessimism may help you to inject wise notes of caution into the wilder plans and projects of your more optimistic colleagues.

Values

What you value is by definition extremely important to you. Your fundamental values guide your behaviour, or protest at it, in all aspects of your life. If you do a job which is constantly at odds with your values it will sooner or later become a burden, a penance or just a terrible bore. The effects of this will carry over into the rest of your life and may turn you into an embittered individual, unappreciated by friends and family. You need to get out of such employment. Here is a small example from my own experience.

Today is Wednesday so it must be Brussels

I once worked for a tour operating company as Tours Planning Manager, an overly grand title that kept my salary low. I was asked by the Managing Director to see whether some of the cheaper coach trips run by a subsidiary company could be improved. On investigation I discovered these trips to be as bad an example of 'Today is Wednesday so it must be Brussels' as I had seen or have seen since.

I suggested to the boss of the coach tour subsidiary that she make a number of minor changes to cut down the length of travelling time between some of the overnight stops. She rejected my proposals completely. When I protested that no one would ever book another tour after such a rushed experience, she said, 'It doesn't matter. They're cheap tours. At those prices there is always another mug.' This was in straightforward conflict with my ideas about good design and giving value for money and a significant contributory reason towards my decision eventually to leave the company.

On the positive side it is perhaps worth adding that firms who set out to provide cheap (they might prefer 'affordable') goods or services, which by definition are not of the highest available quality, are often aware and proud of providing a valuable service to people who otherwise might have to do without them.

Nowadays I would expect most corporate websites to provide some strong clues about how organisations see themselves in terms of values. If, however, you have still not gained a clear idea by the second interview you can simply ask: 'How would you sum up the organisation's values?'

Abilities and experience

I have run these together because experience is the place where we find our abilities. Sometimes clients have asked me to help them discover their latent abilities or hidden talents, on the basis that these have never been used but are somehow lying dormant within them. I cannot think of a single client where this has been the case. They have always used them but 'as yet' in unrecognised ways.

Achievements as a source of abilities

What frequently occurs is that people either do not recognise their own abilities, or believe they are unremarkable, or common to all. There is more about all this in connection with CV writing in Appendix I. The experience which helps you identify your abilities is the experience of achieving things. Not world records or reducing company costs by 50% but anything you have done which gave you satisfaction and which privately at least you feel you did well. Anything will do.

Here is something lots of people will have done:

Building a pergola in the garden (a classic approach)

1. I *consulted* my wife and *agreed* an overall design.

2. I *measured* the area and *made a plan*.

3. I *worked out* how much wood I needed in the different dimensions and how many nails of different sizes.

4. I *ordered* the wood and the nails.

5. I *looked up* in a manual the best sort of joints to make.

6. I *laid* my materials *out in order* of use and *cut* the timber *according to the plan*.

7. I *cut the joints carefully* and *assembled* all the pieces of timber.

8. I *nailed* them *together*.

9. I *tidied up* the site. My wife agreed it looked great.

The italicised words (the verbs or **what he did**) represent the potential abilities of the pergola builder, perhaps:

◆ planning
◆ researching
◆ working to a plan.

In fact **I** built a pergola recently and **my** achievement follows.

Building a pergola (my style)

1. I *gave in* to my wife and *promised* to rebuild the pergola.

2. I *persuaded* her we could use some old oak timbers we had stored in the barn.

3. I *guessed* we would have enough and *visualised* how it might fit.

4. I *realised* a very practical friend was shortly coming to stay and *reckoned* I could *persuade* him to help.

5. He *agreed* to help.

6. I *found* seven timbers of which six were OK and *rescued* some old bent nails.

7. I *told* him my plan (to *re-create* the old pergola) and *asked* him how best to marry the timbers.

8. Under his instruction I *cut the joints by eye*. (They fitted more or less.)

9. I *showed* my wife the finished result. She was amazed and impressed, but told me to clear up the mess.

It reveals a completely different set of potential abilities, perhaps:

◆ persuading
◆ visualising
◆ adapting.

Your plan would doubtless be different again. Think of anything you have made or assembled and write down the steps you took in the process.

Achievements at work are usually easier to relate to readily saleable abilities and may be taken also from projects where you played only a part in the achievement. Your personal contribution is the bit you need to mine for abilities.

Preferences

We also have preferences. Most people have a number of very clear preferences about how they like to perceive the world and how they like to make judgements. I refer here specifically to the Jungian theory of personality types used by Katharine C Briggs and Isabel Briggs Myers as the basis for creating the Myers Briggs Type Indicator* (MBTI) assessment tool, a fascinating and valuable means of understanding the work implications of our individual preferences. The MBTI instrument is one of legions of so called psychometric tests – it is more properly described as a personality inventory – and within its clearly defined limitations amongst the best. (See Appendix II for more details.)

It is important to remember that any means of identifying personality traits does not imprison you in some set manner of behaviour. Frequently an individual does not fit neatly within the 'type'. Also we all remain responsible for our choices and are free therefore to act against type.

*Myers-Briggs Type Indicator and MBTI are registered trade marks of CPP Inc.

Another element to identify is your key 'driver' or 'drivers'. What do you really want to achieve? What motivates you? Interesting work based on Professor Edgar Schein's theory of career anchors has identified nine distinct career drivers, each one being a blend of wants and needs. The nine are:

- material reward
- power and influence
- search for meaning
- expertise
- creativity
- affiliation
- autonomy
- security
- status.

These drivers are held to be basic components of individual identity. (See Appendix II for more details.)

If you have difficulty working out what career path you should follow you will need help, ideally from an experienced career counsellor. Ultimately however **you** will be doing the hard work, whomever you go to for help. You need to think, talk and probably write about your working life in detail, the good bits and the not so good.

How do others see you?

How would your boss describe you to his or her boss? How would your peers describe you to a new colleague joining the organisation? How would people reporting to you describe you to their partners or friends away from work? You are likely to get only partial, possibly less than truthful, answers if you ask all these people such questions, but they are worth asking yourself and considering what the answers might be. There is always more you can find out about yourself and it is usually easier to set about it with a third party.

If you cannot find, or afford, a suitable professional career adviser, coach, counsellor or consultant, use your friends; include your partner or spouse if you have one. Two or three people who know you well, and whose general opinion you respect, can give you valuable insights if asked the right questions. (See Exercises in Appendix IV.)

In asking questions of yourself you might start with the following list:

◆ Who am I?

◆ What have I done?

◆ What is wrong with where I am?

◆ What am I good at?

◆ What am I good at that I **enjoy** doing**?**

◆ Who might want to employ someone like me?

◆ What am I prepared to trade off?

◆ What must I avoid at all costs?

◆ What direction do I want to take?

◆ What would I **really** like to do?

You may not be able to answer all of these now. By the time you get to the end of this book and have done some serious work you should be able to. Whenever you can answer most of them you will be ready to make a start dealing with what for many is the key question:

How do I make this next career move?

Some elements can come only from you. You need **some** talent, the will and the patience to identify other people's needs as well as your own, and a good deal of **persistence.**

Find yourself a label

However you go about discovering all of the above, including **skills, abilities, drivers, experience,** etc, you will need to assemble from these elements some kind of 'label' for yourself. Forget the idea that labels are bad. This only applies when someone else attaches a label to you. This label is going to be carefully crafted by you to fit the needs of your next career move; it will also be true, as far as it goes. There is a tendency for us to remain stuck with what we have been or been doing in life. It is quite easy for someone to start a self-description with 'A qualified solicitor...' having forgotten that she or he is about to give up the law to try to become a hospital manager or whatever. One of my favourite labels was produced by an ex-client who managed to extract the maximum help from a past occupation by starting with 'An escaped academic' thereby claiming enterprise and brains in quick succession.

Ideally you need to find something which either goes to the core of you or which is unusual in some way; if it does both it's a bonus. It may be extremely simple. If you are an international patent lawyer looking for a new job as an international patent lawyer, you've got your first four words. Otherwise more thought will be needed. The same person wanting to make a career change might start with any of a number of different labels, each accurate as far as it goes:

◆ 'A fluent French speaker, with a legal background...'

◆ 'A practised negotiator with fluent French...'

◆ 'An international civil servant, with a background in patent law...'

◆ 'A hardworking and reliable individual...'

What follows will be skills and abilities or maybe a description of the role sought depending on the context. Your 'label' will appear on your CV, in letters and in conversation both formal and informal.

This label will need to expand in order to describe you to others on paper or electronically or face to face. It is all part of the business of finding focus. Even if you know what you want to do in terms of a role, you may not have identified the ideal size, location and culture of organisation you are looking for. The more precise your fix on the career move you want to make, the easier it is to find – assuming it exists at all.

There are two good ways of finding focus. Firstly by reading newspaper, magazine, trade press and Internet job advertisements assiduously. You need to look at the words that the advertisers use (see exercises in Appendix IV). Secondly by networking – see Chapter 3.

Before going much further you need to understand how the market works.

The 'job market'

A useful way of thinking about job search is to use the analogy of a marketplace, where there are buyers and sellers. Crudely put you are **selling** your skills, and employers are **buying** labour to help them survive and prosper. But job search works both ways round. Employers also search for people. When you appreciate this you can start to take control of your own job search properly. It means **making yourself known** where employers can find you – in the **job marketplace.** It may be only a virtual marketplace but many of the features of ordinary markets can be found there – supply and demand effects on prices, negotiating, importance of goods display, people 'just looking', etc.

By understanding how employers conduct their search you can carry out the best possible campaign of your own and meet them in the marketplace.

Job search methods

Once you know, precisely or approximately, how you want your career to develop you can begin your job search. There are five routes.

- networking
- advertised jobs
- recruitment companies
- direct approaches to employers
- advertise yourself.
    (This last is mainly for the self-employed, but is now also used, especially on the net by skilled technicians, to look for contract jobs. Unless you **know** your skills are in great demand and scarce, it is probably a waste of time – but see Appendix III. Also, if your skills are in demand, both the press and the net will be full of advertisements seeking them.)

The fact is that most people do not do much searching. In most cases 'job search' is a misnomer, where the activity implied in the word search is limited to turning the pages of the appointments sections in the press or clicking the mouse at the computer. What they are doing is waiting for someone to place an ad in the press for a position, which would match their abilities and aspirations. They are waiting for others to find them. Waiting will be forced upon you often enough during the job search process. Useful activity is generally better for you.

The buyers

Employers, who are in buying mode:

- network
- advertise in the press
- engage recruitment companies
- read direct approach letters with interest
- **sometimes** look for specialists on the web.

The seller

You therefore need to:

◆ get yourself known on their network

◆ scour the advertisements and respond intelligently

◆ get on the books of as many recruitment companies as possible

◆ write letters direct to organisations you might work for or with

◆ scour the web.

Summary

◆ Get to know yourself better, especially what you are good at.

◆ Find out what motivates you and try to accommodate your preferences.

◆ Look at your achievements. They reveal important things about you.

◆ What is your style? How do you like to do things?

◆ Take account of how others see you. Perceptions are real even when 'wrong'.

◆ Find yourself a label you like that others can recognise.

◆ Appreciate how the market works and what employers are looking for.

CHAPTER TWO

Your Main Marketing Tool

This chapter addresses CV construction and sets out the purposes and essential elements of a modern CV in relation to what the job market demands and to what you want it to do for you. It emphasises the importance of keeping control of your CV and of keeping it brief. It shows you how to create a brief CV from a full version. At the end of the chapter there are examples of CVs that have worked well for others. It points to Appendix I for detailed recommendations on how to write your own CV.

You are marketing yourself in a competitive world so you should take advantage of as many methods as are feasible. For this you will need some basic tools, the most important of which is a CV that you can be proud of and comfortable with.

The origin of the CV

The CV or Curriculum Vitae was an invention of the British Foreign and Commonwealth Office at a time of rapid expansion of the Foreign Service, which had earlier been small enough for those at the top to know where and roughly when their friends and relations had held posts. Suddenly Lord Silverspoon was no longer sure whether young 'Bunny' Nevill had already done a stint in India or not, or whether Archie Fitzffrench spoke any French. The command went out 'Write it all down' and the CV was born. It was simply a chronological record of postings, and its use rapidly spread through the civil service. Today the CV serves different purposes.

Purposes of a modern CV

Its first purpose is **to promote you** in the eyes of potential employers or people who might be able to help you in your job search.

Its second purpose is **to supply selected, factual and useful data** about you to the same people.

There is no conflict between these purposes and there is no other purpose. Indeed the best way to promote yourself in a CV is by selecting true information about yourself that is relevant to the needs of a desired employer, i.e. the kind who needs your talents and experience.

There are certain **essential elements,** which every CV needs. These are:

- Who you are and how to make contact with you.
- What you have to offer, skills, abilities, etc.
- What you have achieved for other employers.
- Some indication of your educational background.
- Some personal information.

1. **Who you are.** If you are and wish to be known as Bob Taylor, don't head your CV with Robert Anthony St John Taylor. Titles and 'letters' such as FCA are used less and less but there are good arguments for using them on occasion. Do put a secure e-mail address as well as your home address.

2. **What you have to offer.** Straightforward language to express **what** you are good at – **not** how good you are at it. Others must judge that.

3. **What you have achieved.** Contributions and differences made in previous employments – crucial evidence to reassure the reader and support your skills and abilities.

4. **Some educational background.** 'Too much' education may be worse than 'too little'. The former can bore people or intimidate them whilst the latter makes your other achievements the more admirable. If, as many people do, you feel your education is lacking find a course to attend and mention it on your CV. Self-improvement is like 'Momma and apple pie'. You just cannot go wrong.

5. **Some personal information.** You are more than a 1984 worker unit. Interviewers often like icebreakers and whilst no one can expect others to share their interests, when people do it creates an extra small bond. Do include passions of any kind. I recall a client who put down under 'Interests' – lawnmower racing, a fascinating and vibrant sport with a sophisticated rule book based on motor racing and at least one annual 'grand prix' race meeting.

Fortunately in the UK we have not remained true to the original meaning of the Latin 'curriculum vitae'. The Germans have not wavered and still demand a 'Lebenslauf', (as the Latin literally your 'life's course'), an umpteen page document to be submitted, charting your progress chronologically from elementary school to the present day. With CVs **'less is more'**. It really is better to leave your reader wanting more, and the less you provide the higher can be its overall quality level.

How many CVs do you need?

Some career counsellors recommend carefully amending a basic core CV or even writing a separate CV for each job application. I strongly disagree. If your CV is to portray **you** then it cannot change much anyway over the course of a few weeks or months. If you keep chopping and changing bits it will rapidly get out of shape, you will forget what you wrote when and sent to whom and you will struggle to remember who you are. This is not to say that you should **never** change your CV. You may receive useful comments from networking acquaintances, which inspire you to make changes. There may be an achievement story, which you have not included in your CV but which would be particularly relevant to a job for which you want to apply; make space for it!

You need one CV which responds to a requirement for a 'full CV', and one which meets a requirement for a 'brief CV'. A single two-page CV can sometimes meet both needs. Most people however will want two or three pages for the full version and you should cut this down to one page for a short CV.

There is also a concept around that good CVs get people jobs and that therefore you need a 'power CV' (whatever that is), or a CV packed with 'action' words to get you the job. All this rather misses the point. A good CV **might** help to get you an interview, but never a job.

The fact is that CVs are not often very closely read; frequently they are only skimmed, especially by readers of job applications. The reason for this is important to understand. At such a time the reader of your CV is looking for applications to reject. When s/he has 200–300 sitting on the desk the more quickly this number can be reduced to 30–40 the better. Almost anything will do: – too long, difficult to understand, something negative? – **Out!**

As indicated above your CV should be a marketing document designed to promote you. Almost always it will be accompanied if not by you then by some kind of covering letter. Another way for you to think about your CV is to appreciate that it has to substitute for you in your absence. You therefore want it to be a rounded document, which shows you as a whole person demonstrating some suitability for the career move you want to make.

Whatever you do with your CV make sure it describes **you**, you as you believe yourself to be on your best days. Check with a good friend if you are not sure. It is absolutely vital that you are comfortable with what it says, and that you are prepared to defend any sentence in it.

In job search as in life, when you are trying to communicate something you have to consider the reader. You must make it as easy as possible for him/her to find their way through your document, using appropriate 'signposts', clear headings, leaving white space around headings and sections, with a minimum number of different type faces and styles.

At the end of this chapter there are examples of CVs that have worked well. Detailed instructions on how to put one together are to be found in Appendix I.

The brief CV

Such an item may be called for in a job advertisement. It is also strongly recommended as the appropriate form of CV to send when making unsolicited approaches to recruitment agencies, and may also be used with other unsolicited approaches. (See Chapter 5 for unsolicited approaches.) It is most easily achieved by taking the blue pencil to your full CV. The aim is to get it down to one page of A4. This will leave enough space for:

◆ Name, address, etc.

◆ Objective (description of job sought), if you have one.

◆ Profile, pen portrait including key strengths, (3–5 lines).

◆ Career to date over last 10–15 years (half the page) – contributions/ achievements.

- Highest relevant educational/training achievement/qualification.

- Personal details/interests (1–2 lines).

Your CV is an important complementary and supplementary aid to a letter or to your physical presence. Other uses for CVs are of only marginal benefit. You may attach your CV to an application form provided you are not specifically requested **not** to do so. Employers and recruiters, on writing to advise you that your application has not been successful, may request your indulgence in allowing them to retain your CV in their filing system against some future recruitment need. No harm done but no need to get excited either.

Occasionally people may ask for a copy of your CV to show to someone else. Simply handing one over is almost certainly a mistake. You need to know why your CV might be needed and you will probably want to meet this person anyway. It is a typical problem arising when people want to help you **too much**. The thinking goes something like this.

> I wonder if Michael could use someone like this. I know he has employed people in strategic jobs, but I'm not sure whether he's actually looking for anyone at the moment. It might be a wild goose chase, and I don't want to get this person's hopes up if it's a dead end. But Michael might look at the CV, and it is in the right business area. If he's got a suitable job he might be interested in a meeting.

The corollary is that if Michael does not have a suitable job he won't want to see you, and bang goes your networking opportunity. (See Networking and keeping control, Chapter 3, fourth rule, page 47.)

Keep control of your CV and make sure it doesn't go anywhere without an accompanying message and follow-up from you.

Component parts of the CV

1. (Objective): **optional**, the type of role and organisation you seek and your major intended contribution to it.

2. **Profile:** a description of you, a little of your background, and what you can offer an organisation in terms of key strengths and experience.

3. (Career highlights or selected achievements): **optional**, 4/5 brief examples, which illustrate and provide 'proof' of the profile above.

4. **Career details**: a list in reverse order of the positions you have held with dates, showing your achievements or the contributions you have made.

5. **Education and training**: in reverse order, starting with your highest qualification.

6. **Personal details**: date of birth, etc, and interests if not given its own section.

> **A CV should be typed/printed, easy to read, brief (one to three pages), positive and reassuring.**

Various other sections may be relevant between numbers 5 and 6 if they support your cause. (See Appendix I for details on how to write your own.) See pp 25–33 for some CVs that have worked.

Summary

- ◆ Your CV should promote you honestly to employers and others who can help you.

◆ Keep it brief; select the facts; less is more.

◆ It needs to describe you as an individual. People buy people.

◆ It must be clearly laid out and easy to read.

◆ Keep control of who does what with your CV.

A well balanced 3-page 'full CV'

Telephone: (H) 01932 xxx123   12 Lesley Drive
            (M) 077xx 123456   Richmond
e-mail anna@mcdougal.maestra.net   Surrey GT4 12SD

ANNA MCDOUGAL

OBJECTIVE

A senior consultancy role where my communication, planning and people skills will contribute directly to the development of people and business performance.

PROFILE

A highly creative and disciplined manager who values human resources and who has eight years' experience of marketing in product and service companies. Key strengths include:

◆ Using a simple and logical approach to communicate information clearly.
◆ Comprehensive knowledge of IT planning tools and applications.
◆ Getting the best out of people by focusing on their needs and motivation.
◆ Solving problems by quickly establishing root causes.

SOME ACHIEVEMENTS

Handling the first TQM project at HNZ Groceries
Faced with this task the team lacked confidence and cohesion. As project leader I encouraged both individual contribution and team co-operation, whilst applying the TQM process to the problem. The team identified a cost saving of £250k and our recommendations were endorsed at a board presentation.

Minster National's new TESSA
Prepared and delivered presentations, created sales training materials and produced bulletins and videos for circulation throughout the company. In research the 3,000 sales staff confirmed the vital role of the communications package in the success of the launch.

HNZ's first frozen foods
This launch required the co-ordination of internal departments plus advertising, design and PR agencies. Set up three working parties to brief relevant personnel on product development, sales and marketing requirements. These met regularly to review progress and share ideas, thereby ensuring the timing and success of the launch, which won a major retailing award.

CAREER PROGRESSION

CAREER BREAK
Nine months travelling in South East Asia, Australia and USA.

1997–1999   MINSTER NATIONAL PLC

1999   **Marketing Manager – Europe and Offshore**
Set up the overseas marketing function, developing marketing plans and implementing market research projects in Italy, Spain and Jersey.

1997–1999   **Planning Manager – Marketing**
Developed Minster National's financial services range in existing and new markets. Improved position in the £50bn. Savings market with launch of top selling UK TESSA. Undertook four major research projects and created some 20 product concepts for future development.

1994–1997   HNZ GROCERIES LTD

1995–97   **Product Manager – WW Foods**
Managed the expansion of WW foods to a £70m brand including strategic planning, achievement of sales and profit targets, with control of a £7m marketing budget.

1994–95   **Junior Product Manager HNZ Peas**
Assisted in the management of this £150m brand, in charge of new product development, PR, packing design and controlling a £4m marketing budget.

1991–1994   AMALGAMATED BAKERS LTD

1993–94   **Assistant Product Manager – Morning Goods** (Buns, rolls etc.)
In charge of packaging and promotion of the Moonstruck Rolls and Breakfast ranges and for new product development projects.

1991–93   **Management Trainee – Marketing**
Based in the Marketing department gained a broad commercial experience by working in production, sales, R&D and national accounts.

EDUCATION

1987–1991   University of Strathclyde, Glasgow

BSc Hons (2.1) Technology and Business Studies

1981–1987   Baker's High School, Forfar, Scotland

2 CSYs ('S' Level equivalent): English and French
5 'Highers' and 10 'O' Levels

COMMERCIAL & BUSINESS TRAINING

A range of internal training courses at HNZ Groceries Ltd and Minster National including:

- Finance for Non-Financial Managers.
- Effective Sales Promotion.
- Presentation Skills.
- Appraisal Skills.
- Time Management.
- Chairmanship.
- Total Quality Management.
- Project Management.
- Word, Excel, Powerpoint and Internet courses.

LANGUAGES

Conversational French and Italian.

INTERESTS

Dance, travel, food, fitness.

PERSONAL DATA

Single, excellent health, date of birth 30th October 1969

Observations

This could easily be slightly cut and rearranged to become two pages, but as it stands it appears neat and very clear – a good piece of communication from a good communicator.

A full 3-page – it seems a little crowded by comparison – and its derived 'short CV'.

Michael James

9 Wade Avenue, Mapledurham, Southampton, Hants. Tel. 01234 497562

OBJECTIVE

Senior management role, where planning, control, staff motivation and customer relations can be combined with design and innovation to strongly contribute to the efficiency and financial strength of the organisation.

PROFILE

Following comprehensive electrical, electronic and avionics training with the RAF, 21 years of technical, supervisory and management experience, including 10 years in the private sector. Areas of proven ability include:

♦ Project and engineering management – employing careful planning and precise control, directing staff within strict financial and quality guidelines.

♦ Customer relations and negotiation – by keeping up regular communications, to understand, persuade and compromise.

♦ Team leadership – through clear delegation, encouragement and personal example, calm and agile under pressure.

♦ Design and implementation – of building and ground support facilities.

SELECTED ACHIEVEMENTS

Three projects involving complex mechanical assemblies in addition to electronic controls were in difficulty on transfer to my charge. By identifying individual strengths, transferring task responsibilities and by budgetary manipulation, the projects were completed within overall projects costs of over £180k.

Analysis of inherited tasks showed overspend and time slippage on 21 of 230 projects. By providing accurate statistics to client, negotiated additional funding and revised completion dates. This recouped potential losses of £120k and generated additional business of approximately £200k.

At Rediffusion Simulation Ltd responsibilities on my arrival included (on average) some 200 simultaneous projects, a total of 65 clients and some 50 direct and indirect staff. Built and maintained team spirit by involving staff in activities previously confined to management and increased productivity by 15% in first year.

A new radar support facility was required at a remote RAF site. I surveyed the building, produced scale drawings, researched equipment, designed equipment layout, power supplies etc, then planned and supervised the installation to complete on schedule. This was the first of over 30 similar successful projects in a five-year period.

CAREER PROGRESSION

1987–1991 REDIFFUSION LTD, AYLESBURY

Senior Project Manager (19 direct engineers and technical staff, 29 indirect)

High profile client contact, full project and engineering responsibilities for 200 (average) simultaneous hardware and software projects of total value exceeding £3.5m annually. All work to strict quality standards including BS5750 and AQAPS 1 & 13 + TQM. Completed more than 250 projects within agreed times and costs.

1981–1987 GEC AVIONICS LTD, RADLETT

Installations Manager 1983–87 (17 direct mixed trade engineers plus indirect staff)

All aspects of the installation and commissioning of ground support facilities, at client sites and in-house, for the Nimrod AEW aircraft. All due work completed, or within time and budget, at time of cancellation of aircraft project.

Section Leader (1982–83)

Heading team of 5 engineers, coordinated all installation activities with other departmental engineers, sub-contractors and clients building and service contractors, ensuring conformance to rigid specifications and safety practices by all parties.

Senior Electrical Engineer (1981–82)

Total specification and design of all electrical systems to support the aircrew and Ground Controller's major training facilities for Nimrod AEW. Detail included Electromagnetic Compatibility and electronic security measures, access controls, flooring, environmental and fire systems.

1958–1981 ROYAL AIR FORCE

To **Chief Technician**

Trained and practised as Aircraft Fitter (Electrical) with additional training in instrumentation, advanced electronics and avionic systems. Supervisory responsibilities from 1965 and managerial from 1970. Final 5 years: **Project Leader** for the design and installation of military electronics ground support facilities.

1956–58 O'ROURKE'S ENTERTAINMENTS, HASTINGS

Operator and Maintenance Engineer for customer interactive games – had fun!

EDUCATION AND TRAINING

1952–1956   HASTINGS GRAMMAR SCHOOL

1958–1981   RAF

(Intensive courses)

1961–1962   Aircraft Electrical Fitter (= City & Guilds Electrical/Electronic Engineering)

1964   Instrumentation Conversion Course – Advanced Electronics

(Part time)

1963–1979   GCE 'O' Levels: Mathematics, English Language, Physics, Geometric & Mechanical Drawing

LUTON COLLEGE

1985   City and Guilds: 15th Edition of the IEE Wiring Regulations for Electrical Installations.

Other short and part time courses

Man Management	RAF
Communication skills	RAF
PERT Networking	RAF
Project Management	Kepner Tregoe
Electronic Compatibility	Don White Associates

PROFESSIONAL

Member of the Institute of Supervisory Management (M.I.S.M.)

INTERESTS

Sailing – participation on opportunity. Badminton – former club Chairman. Vehicle restoration – welding, shaping, finishing.

PERSONAL DETAILS

Date of birth: 7th February 1941

Married – two grown-up daughters

British nationality

Excellent health

Clean driving licence

A one page version of above that loses very little when reduced from three pages.

Michael James
9 Wade Avenue
Mapledurham
Southampton
Tel. 01234 497562
Hants

PROFILE

A resourceful and competent engineering and project manager with a record of consistent achievement. Wide range of experience and knowledge gained from avionics and defence industries.

OBJECTIVE

A senior management role in a technical environment, with project, engineering and client responsibilities.

CAREER PROGRESSION

REDIFFUSION SIMULATION Ltd
1987–91 **Senior Project Manager**
Costed, planned, controlled continuous turnover of 200 hardware/software projects. Total annual contract value £3.5m+. 19 direct staff, 29 indirect. 250 projects completed in time/costs.

GEC AVIONICS Ltd
1983–87 **Installations Manager**
Full installation responsibilities for Nimrod AEW aircraft ground support facilities. All facilities completed or within time/costs at cancellation.

1982–83 **Section Leader**
Coordinated and supervised all Nimrod AEW support installations.

1981–82 **Senior Electrical Engineer**
Designed all electrical systems and specified building support systems for Nimrod AEW support facilities.

Early career to 1981 with Royal Air Force.

EDUCATION AND QUALIFICATIONS

RAF Education (part time)
GCE O Levels: Maths, English Language, Physics, Geometric and Mechanical Drawing.

RAF Trade Training
C&G Electrical Electronic Engineering (Equivalent)

Luton College
IEE Regulations 15th Edition

Professional: Member of the Institute of Supervisory Management

Personal Details: Married with 2 daughters. Excellent health. D.o.b. 7th Feb 1941

COMPREHENSIVE CV AVAILABLE ON REQUEST

Dual purpose 'brief' or 'full' CV.

01252 465199   12 Johnson Close
peterr@buzz.com   Farnborough Hants
                                                GU7 4PH

PETER REDBRIDGE

OBJECTIVE

A senior financial role in a small to medium sized organisation in which my analytical skills, organising ability and flexibility will contribute to profitable expansion.

PROFILE

A chartered accountant with significant international and group experience, with particular strength in operational control and financial accounting functions. Grasps new concepts quickly, able to combine logical analysis and intuition to establish key information from a mass of data. A team player with well developed spoken and written communication skills.

CAREER PROGRESSION

2000–2003   THE COLONIAL TOBACCO COMPANY LTD

      02–03   Ghanaian Subsidiary – t/o £25m
Financial Controller
Redesigned the whole financial reporting system, reducing quantity by 50% and improving quality of information provided.

      00–01   UK Subsidiary – t/o £400m
Head of Internal Audit
Recruited to regenerate the UK audit function. Rebuilt department to audit activities in 5 UK profit centres and some 15 overseas locations.

1998–2000   MAGIPART GROUP OF COMPANIES – t/o £350m
Audit Manager
Headed the operational audit section of the internal audit department. Key member of team to investigate despatch error rates. These fell over 9 mth period from 5% to 1.5% on order lines of over 1 million car parts per annum.

1997–1998   JOHNSON BROTHERS MERCHANT BANK
Accountant – Unit Trust Accounting Department
Reconstructed accounting records and drafted interim and final Unit Trust accounts statements for publication.

1994–97	WHEELERS & DEALERS, Harare, Zimbabwe.

95–97	**Senior Consultant**

Ran various consultancy projects for such organisations as Chloride Batteries, the Zimbabwe Broadcasting Corporation and the Zimbabwe Tax Department.

94–95	**Audit Senior**

1989–1994	BEAN COUNTERS, Bury St Edmunds.
	Articled Clerk

EDUCATION

1985–1989	Edinburgh University
	BA in Business Administration

1979–1985	Boddingtons Grammar School, Nr Forfar
	9 CSE 'O' Levels
	6 SCE 'Higher' Levels

PROFESSIONAL QUALIFICATION

Chartered Accountant – qualified 1993

LEISURE INTERESTS

Squash	Cricket
Travel	Music

PERSONAL DATA

Date of birth	:	24th May 1967
Marital status	:	Married, no children
Health	:	Excellent

CHAPTER THREE

The Best Way – Networking

'Networking' unveiled. This is a comprehensive description of the principles and practices of networking as applied to making a career move and how it can help to gain tighter focus on the next move. It shows how job opportunities arise and takes the fear and pressure out of the process. It explains not only how and why it works but also addresses how to deal with the many different people and situations you will encounter. It also lists the rules to be followed and what to avoid.

At the end of the chapter there are samples of the various types of letter, which need to be written in the course of networking and examples of networking successes.

What is networking?

Many people dread the idea of 'networking'. They associate it with the old boy network attached to British public schools, or think of it as asking people for favours, or somehow exploiting others. It has nothing to do with any of this.

Networking in the context of job search **is about meeting people** operating in the area of work which interests you **to collect** the **information** you need to help you find a suitable job **and about broadcasting your availability and suitability**. Clearly you are asking for help from others. If it is the kind of help you would happily give you will get it also from others.

More people find jobs by being on someone's network than by any other method, and it is within his/her own network that **the employer starts the search.**

Most jobs go to internal appointees who are already on the internal network, and typically, say when someone retires from a senior role, two or three promotions may be made making way for one new person recruited at a junior level. On other occasions a new function is incorporated into an existing employee's job, and the need to recruit is avoided – usually the preferred option for an employer.

When neither of these outcomes is possible or desirable the employer starts to scratch his/her head and tries to think of some friend, acquaintance or ex-colleague who could do the job. If this yields no result the would-be employer will usually ask a few friends or colleagues whether they can think of anyone who might be suitable for the role.

Why start this way? There are at least three reasons.

- ◆ Time may be saved in making an appointment.
- ◆ The cost of formal recruitment procedures would be saved.
- ◆ Someone known of, and thought to be potentially suitable, carries

connotations of familiarity and hence safety and trust. The **connection** that is already in place has a value in itself.

In most cases the last is the most important and is always present as a reason.

Focus and your functional role

Ideally you know exactly the sort of job you want to do, the sector, location(s) and approximate size of the organisation in which you want to do it. You can therefore work out rapidly which organisations might be interested in employing you at some stage and start the process of networking, approaching suitable agencies and writing to companies direct. Not everyone is in this fortunate position however.

If you do not have this kind of focus but do know what you are good at and enjoy doing, you need at least to be able to define the **functional** role you would like to make the core of your working life. Here are some examples:

> I want a job in which I can use my intuition, my creativity and my ability to listen to people to help them make good decisions for themselves. I would also be interested to explore with people their thoughts and feelings and help them make sense of whatever currently does not.

Or

> I want a job in which I can use my ability to motivate people to achieve better performance using my natural enthusiasm and energy, and where I can identify key issues, build relationships and, using my presentation skills, sell ideas to people and generate useful profit for the company.

(Having written this statement the backroom project engineer concerned still needed to be told by others that perhaps he should make a career move into sales or marketing – which he did.)

Or

> I want a job in which I can use my research and analytical abilities and my ability to construct detailed plans, which others will implement. I want to use my financial modelling skills and experience of forecasting techniques at the macro-economic level. I would prefer a public sector role.

About fifty words should be enough. This statement could be your answer to the question: *What would make you happy in your career?* (One of the questions a friend might have answered if you have followed the recommendations in Appendix IV.) The above statements derive from a simple list of the **abilities** of each person concerned, sometimes with the addition of a skill or some experience.

If you have this degree of definition it is more than enough to start networking. In the process of identifying and learning about jobs, which require the skills and abilities you want to use in your work, you will acquire sharper focus. And as you do so you can meet and become known to more people in the right areas. You will also find out how much your talents are in demand and roughly or, precisely in some cases, what they are worth.

Why is networking the best way?

What makes it the best method is a combination of things. Firstly, it is the natural starting point and preferred method of employers. Secondly, it is the least competitive method; when potential jobs are discovered through networking only two or three people are likely to be under consideration alongside you. Thirdly, you have a real possibility of influencing the shape and scope of the job so that it fits your abilities and needs as closely as possible.

How to do it

This rarely taught discipline needs to be thought about and done properly. If you follow the basic rules it will work well and become interesting and enjoyable. If you cut corners your networking will fail.

Networking is the most powerful and widely used job-finding method and addresses directly the so-called 'unadvertised job market'. It is the naturally preferred method of manual workers and top executives, but widely misunderstood and misused by clerical, administrative, middle and senior management people. The unadvertised job market, often described by career counselling firms as if it were a secret list of jobs to which they alone have access, describes a real enough entity but like the job market as a whole it is only a virtual marketplace.

The unadvertised job market consists of all those jobs that are not advertised by choice, because employers **prefer** to find someone through an existing connection, thereby having a sort of recommendation by association. To this total should be added all those jobs that are not yet defined but which define themselves around a person encountered through an existing connection. This includes jobs about to be advertised or put out to recruitment companies, when suddenly a suitable candidate walks in the door. Many jobs are long in gestation. Months can elapse between there being a **need** to employ someone and recognition of that need and translation of it into a position with a clear job description. Many jobs are also not advertised for reasons of secrecy; there may be people inside or outside the organisation who should not know what is happening.

The basic objectives of networking

- ◆ To make known and present your skills and abilities to people who can help you in your job search.
- ◆ To acquire a sharper degree of focus on your career objectives.
- ◆ To locate potential job opportunities.

Additionally it can be used to target individuals you want to meet.

Everything is connected

All our networks – yours, mine, and that of the President of the USA – are connected, or can be made to connect. When I was first given the exercise of trying to work out how I might find a path through to meet the President, his name was Reagan and the route was fun.

My wife and I had had dinner the previous weekend with an elderly couple in our village, who had themselves been entertained the previous weekend in San Francisco by a couple, who the previous weekend had been entertained by President and Mrs Nancy Reagan at the White House. How about that for an unlikely sequence of events?

It is easier to establish a route to someone at the top of a tree than it is for Joe Bloggs to find Mary Smith. Either of these should be able to reach the US President, should they want to, first via their local MP, who will know a senior British diplomat or member of the government, who knows an American politician or civil servant, who knows the President.

If you want to target someone using the networking process in job search mode, it will usually be someone fairly senior and well known, and you will often find a short route.

Why networking works

- ◆ **The world of work is a world of people.** Organisations and their products, services, survival and profits depend upon the connections and decisions made by people. The same is true of recruitment and restructuring.

- ◆ **People prefer to say 'yes' rather than 'no'.** It is simply much easier and more pleasant for people to be able to say 'yes'. Saying 'no' is likely to upset the other person and extra effort is needed to avoid this. In some cultures, Japanese for instance, saying 'no' is considered almost rude, which explains why the various circumlocutions for it all sound like 'yes'.

◆ **People enjoy honest respect and recognition.** The emphasis here is on honest. People see through flattery and usually do not like it. (What are they being buttered up for? they ask themselves.) Everyone, however, enjoys praise or recognition for achievement or expertise. It doesn't matter how senior they are or how dismissive of it they are on the surface, they all like it. It is self-affirming positive feedback of the best possible kind.

◆ **People like to give advice from a basis of knowledge.** It is easier, especially when talking to someone we do not know, to start inside our comfort zone. It is also enjoyable for most people to be able to demonstrate their knowledge and expertise and to initiate others into new areas. In a real sense it makes people feel important.

◆ **People respond best to a gradual approach.** Put another way people do not like to be 'bounced' (as Rabbit was by Tigger in A. A. Milne's story) or taken by surprise or without warning. When someone has expectations of you or is asking for your help you often need time to ascertain that you can respond positively.

Networking is about gaining knowledge and access to knowledge. Knowledge is power, and knowledge of the most useful kind is in people's heads. We can always do with more, useful knowledge.

Meetings are for networking

If you are serious about making a career move every meeting you hold or find yourself in, which is not a job interview, should either be a network meeting, or provide the opportunity to arrange one.

Remember that people's time is precious. You need to be businesslike and efficient in your approach. All you want from the people you meet is 20–30 minutes of their time. You will often get more.

There are three specific things you can get from people you know:

◆ advice
◆ information
◆ names and addresses of other people, who might help you further in your job search.

At the same time you should leave with them a clear impression of what strengths you have and how you would like to use them in a work context. The people you meet in this way can then become 'listening stations' for you and advise you if they hear of any possible leads.

You know people, who you like and/or respect, who could form part of your network. You do not know everything or everyone they know. This last is a crucial point. You may think that your friend Fred cannot help you, but you may not know that he lives next door to someone who can. Still less do you know whom he might meet tomorrow!

Make a list of **all** the people you can think of: friends, relations, former work colleagues and bosses, fellow members of associations and clubs, professional advisers, lawyers, doctors, ex-customers, ex-suppliers, neighbours, etc. It is important to write down the names as rapidly as possible without stopping to think whether or how useful they might be. The act of writing will trigger forgotten names. **Keep writing until you cannot remember any more names.** All of them potentially have helpful information and advice they can give you if approached in the right way. If you are focused enough to network, i.e. if you know the functional role you want to carry out, you should start this task now.

Never ask for a job

Paradoxically, the last way of finding a job through networking is to ask for one. The reason is straightforward enough. Most of the time there is no suitable job. All that the request does is introduce a negative note, and possibly guilt into the psyche of who you asked this usually embarrassing question. The fact is that people want to help you. If they know of any suitable job they will tell you soon enough.

'Contacts'

A word about this rather ugly word. Never **ask** for 'contacts' in the course of networking; the word is anathema to many people, who naturally enough prefer to be approached for their own wisdom and knowledge rather than for that of people they know. If you think of 'contact' as meaning 'a person with whom **you** have made contact' you will be safe. Other people's contacts are people **they** know, who **may** become contacts of yours at some later date.

The rules for setting up network meetings

I cannot emphasise enough the importance of a disciplined approach to networking. If you are the most charming extravert in the world, without a shy bone in your body, who loves meeting people and do **not** follow the rules you will **not** be as effective as the shyest introvert who **does**.

First – plan the meeting. What information and advice do you expect from the meeting? If you don't know this, should you be having a meeting? Prepare a list of questions.

Second – write a letter, **or** send an **e-mail** if you have specific reason to believe it to be more acceptable, to ask for a meeting. E-mail may be easier for you, but that is not the point. Some very close friends may be telephoned, but **writing a letter is never wrong**. The letter should follow a pattern:

To someone you do not know or know only slightly.

(a) Establish honest respect or esteem for the particular recipient of the letter. 'I am writing to you because you know a lot about...' / 'you helped me with...'. If the person is a contact given you by someone else, refer to that other person – 'Mr B suggested I write to you because...' Remember that it is the strength of the connection with Mr B which will make your meeting possible, rather than anything to do with you.

or

To someone you know or have known well.

(a) Establish, if some time has elapsed, when and in what circumstances you last met and any major news you might have since then. Say that you want his/her help.

The rest of the letter applies to anyone.

(b) Refer to enclosing your CV 'for background information'. Refer to the fact that you are seeking to 'advance your career'/'establish a new career direction'/'find a new job', whatever is true for you. (People have difficulty with this very simple element often believing that it gives the game away, by which they mean 'it shows you are really after a job'. **This is indeed mostly the case, and there is neither need nor reason to hide it.** Hence the importance of the disclaimer that follows.)

(c)* Reassure the person you are writing to with a clear disclaimer: '**I do not expect you to have a job for me or know of any job opportunities**'. There is no conflict between this statement and the fact that you want to make a career move. Be sensible about this disclaimer. There are many people you will see who could not possibly have a job for you, and it looks silly to state something so obvious. Anyone however could **know of** an opportunity so you always need to disclaim **that** as an expectation.

*This is the most important message of your letter, and nothing works as well as the word '**expect**'. You **must** also believe the message yourself. It is important because you need the recipient to feel fully able to accommodate your request. You must not worry him/her about somehow having to supply some good job leads. That is **not** the point of the letter. You are looking for information and advice.

(d) Establish the purpose of the meeting, e.g. to obtain information/to discuss job market areas which interest you. Be specific whenever possible; you want to ask for help which can be seen to be deliverable. Phrases such as 'advice on developing my career' are wrong because they are too broad.

(e) Acknowledge the value of the person's time and say that you will call in a few days time to set up a brief meeting. This allows you to keep control and absolves him/her from having to do anything.

(For examples of letters setting up networking meetings see the end of this chapter.)

Third – make a telephone call, referring to your letter, and be prepared to repeat that you do not expect your contact to know of any current openings. Focus on when you might conveniently meet – this is the purpose of the call.

Friends and ex-colleagues will normally see you without raising any difficulties. People you have not met may have forgotten your letter, not read it properly, or simply be distracted by their own immediate work concerns. Identify yourself. Remind them of the name of the person who referred you to them and why the referral was made. Suggest two specific dates and have your diary to hand. **Don't** start the meeting on the phone – if you do that is where it will finish.

Secretaries and other gatekeepers

If the person you have contacted is out or otherwise unavailable find out when would be a suitable time to call back. If asked the purpose of your call, say that you have written a letter and that your call is expected; do not agree to be called back, you will ring again. Be polite but firm and make an ally of the 'gatekeeper'; get their name so you can ask for them next time. Keep control and keep trying; busy people are usually worth seeing.

Fourth – hold the meeting, anything from 15 minutes to an hour plus can be ideal. You will have planned and called the meeting, and the contact will expect you to have an agenda for it.

The overall purpose is to gather advice and information to help you in your job search so start by repeating this. Thank your contact for seeing you, referring if relevant to the help and opinion received from the person who gave you the contact's name. If you have a clear job objective state what it is. If not, you might say, 'I am currently researching areas where I can use my sales skills and experience in Europe. Mr X told me that you have a wide knowledge of the European chemical industry and would be able to tell me a great deal about it'. Tell your contact a bit about yourself and your strengths or describe the functional role you seek.

Then get the person talking about what he or she knows by asking appropriate questions.

- How did you get to your current position?

- Which sectors in your industry are likely to show long-term growth?

- Which areas would you suggest I explore?

- Which headhunters or agencies have you used? You may get an introduction.

People you meet in this process may tell you that specific obstacles lie in your way. Enlist their help. If they don't know the solution, they may 'know a (wo)man who does'.

One of the main purposes of the meeting is to get names and addresses of other people who might give you further advice and information. Often these will emerge naturally in the course of discussion. However, you should explain that you are trying to get to see as many people as possible. If no names have emerged at or towards the end of your meeting you should ask if she or he could think of one or two people who could give further advice or information specific to your conversation. Some people on your network-to-be will ask for time to think of names or may express a wish to talk to them first. This is fine. But do reassure them that you will not be expecting their contacts to know of specific job opportunities either. **Stay in control** by saying you will ring them in a few days, or a week or so.

> **DANGER:**
>
> Resist strongly suggestions that a contact send your CV to a few people who might be interested. Say something like ' It would be even more helpful if I could write to them direct. They probably don't have an opening which would suit me, or even know of one elsewhere, but at least I might be able to spend half an hour or so with them and find out more about what is happening industry-wide. I should hate to miss that opportunity'. *If you do not react in some such fashion, the potential extension to your network will surely not materialise.*

Fifth (and most important of all) – after the meeting write a thank you letter.

Everyone gets a thank you letter, or an e-mail (you will know by now if this is acceptable). Write within 24 hours and be specific in your thanks. Mention something in your conversation which you found particularly useful. It is not only courteous to send a thank you letter but it has practical value for you.

♦ As a fresh reminder it may trigger immediate, extra useful information.

♦ It registers you as a courteous person who appreciates the help given.

♦ It makes them feel good about themselves.

♦ It makes any future contact you may make that much more welcome.

♦ It reinforces long-term memory, so if they hear of a possible job...

If you network well you may be given the names of more people than you have time to follow up, but it is a good problem to have. You will just have to be selective.

Summary of the rules of networking

1. Plan the meeting.

2. Write a letter.

3. Follow up by telephone.

4. Conduct the meeting.

5. **Send a thank you letter.**

The network meeting agenda

It is your responsibility to have an agenda; you called the meeting. You will find that network meetings do not always follow a pattern, however well organised you are, but try to include the following elements.

♦ **Establishing rapport** – Take enough time for this. Set the scene.
  – Thank him or her for seeing you.
  – Pass on regards/message from whoever introduced you.
  – Introduce yourself.
  – Explain your purpose – specific objective or options being researched.
  – Describe the sort of help you are looking for.
  – Describe what stage you are at in your job search.
  – Make a firm disclaimer you are **not expecting** a job from or via contact.
  – Talk about your abilities.
  – Get the other person talking. 'How did you get into pig farming?'

♦ **Getting advice**
  – What **options** are there for you in other fields?
  – Ask how you can best use your abilities.
  – Listen for potential contact names (make a note for later, when you can get addresses, check spellings, etc)
  – Ask about salary range.
  – Equire about age and experience factors.

– What qualifications are needed?

– Ask them to check your **CV** for clarity and balance, presentation, content and style. Ask for their reaction if it were presented for a job. (Be careful here, everyone is a CV 'expert'. You can waste a lot of time.)

◆ **Information about the job market** – the real one that interests you.

◆ **Sources of information about jobs.**

– The net, good websites, directories, appropriate trade press.

– **Recruitment** – methods, agencies known, industry practices.

– **State of the market,** good and bad areas, good and bad companies, growth and decline.

– **People,** industry experts, ex-colleagues, mentors, customers, suppliers.

◆ **Information about potential network contacts**. Ask about relationships. There is only one sure reason why a complete stranger should be prepared to give you half an hour of their time, altruism apart. Someone whom they like and or respect has suggested the meeting. You need to know what sort of person this potential contact is, what the connection is and how well acquainted these people are. **This is vital information for planning the next meetings.**

◆ **Leave a good impression**. At the end of your meeting you should thank your new contact for any advice, information and names of people to contact you have obtained. You may promise to let them know how your job search works out. **If you do this, be sure to do so.** Now thank them for the meeting.

Afterwards – write a thank you letter.

Kuala Lumpur here I come. . .

My favourite networking success story features a man of 36, married with two small children, who was very keen to get a job, preferably but not necessarily in project management, with a hi-tech company somewhere on the Pacific Rim. Ideal would be Kuala Lumpur, where he had spent a few years once before.

He had been very reluctant to do any networking, preferring to spend his time chasing every advertised job which came anywhere near to any of his requirements, and harrying agencies constantly. He had been doing this for six months and had had interviews but never for the right job. I had made several efforts to get him to change his approach but without success.

He and his family were going up to Manchester for the weekend to visit his mother-in-law. 'No networking this weekend, then,' said I, hinting feebly. 'No. I'm afraid not,' he replied, deadpan. Two weeks later he told me this story over the telephone.

'You'll be pleased to hear I've landed my job. When I went up to see my mother-in-law two weeks ago, she asked me what sort of job I was after. Was it in telecoms, she said. I said near enough. Then she mentioned this new next-door neighbour, a ''nice young man who worked for Mortal'' she thought. Why didn't I have a chat with him? So I had to really.

'Anyway, he put me onto his boss's boss, who worked in Leeds. We had a very interesting discussion. I really liked him, and he told me what he knew of Nortel's and other companies' activities out on the Pacific Rim. I wrote to thank him and two days later had a call from a senior guy from Nortel in London. He mentioned my meeting in Leeds and would I come and have a chat?

'It didn't feel like an interview but he talked about a possible job in Kuala Lumpur in bid management, possibly leading to a project management job. Over the weekend I had two telephone interviews with the General Manager in KL, my boss to be. I've been a bit busy since then, and we are flying out, the whole family, this Thursday. I start work on Monday!'

There are several things I like about this story. Everything happened miraculously fast. It turned out that the London Nortel Senior Executive had only just heard about the new position in KL, and had casually mentioned it to the man in Leeds just **after** the latter met my client. Another nice feature of the story is that it starts with his mother-in-law, chatting over the garden fence. **(Don't forget your family in the networking process.)** The story turns, however, on four little words in the last paragraph but one above, 'I really liked him.' The feeling was obviously mutual, and it was this that led directly to the crucial discussions in London and with KL. Ultimately it worked of course because my client had the abilities and experience that Nortel needed.

I suppose what I really liked about the story was that, albeit almost by accident, he had proved me right in my attempts to get him networking. But I didn't crow – much.

Summary

- Networking is meeting people to collect information and to broadcast your availability and talents.

- Start with people you like and/or respect.

- You can use networking to find focus, to sharpen focus and to find new options.

- There are rules for networking which are not for breaking.

- Remember that you are not **expecting** job leads from people you meet.

- Remember to send everyone a thank you letter.

A genuine networking star

I have known many networking stars, one of who is the man mentioned in Chapter 1 who dubbed himself 'an escaped academic'. He quickly learned effective networking skills and set out to find more than one job to ensure variety. He found three, which he dovetailed neatly together. One of them grew out of this simple networking letter.

Kenneth Reed was someone met through networking, and when, after the meeting with Christopher James, Simon telephoned him to say he had been offered a job Ken was astonished.

Christopher James
Editorial Director
Dogwood Publishing
14 Warsaw Avenue
London N1 7RZ
                                        April 14th 1999

Dear Mr James

I was speaking with Kenneth Reed recently and he suggested I should contact you. Ken tells me that you have considerable experience and expertise in magazine publishing and would be able to provide me with helpful and constructive advice.

My current situation is that I have had a successful career in STM publishing and am now seeking to use my abilities and acquired skills in a new publishing environment.

Please understand that I am not expecting you to know of any available positions. I am just seeking to broaden my knowledge of magazine publishing and would very much welcome the opportunity of hearing how things work, or not, from your perspective.

I would be most grateful if we could meet for twenty minutes or so to discuss these issues and will telephone you shortly to arrange a convenient date. In the meantime I enclose a copy of my CV for your information.

I am looking forward very much to meeting you.

Yours sincerely

Dr Simon Stoddart

Letters fit for the purpose (networking)

Some are stolen from my clients and are different from each other in style; others are made up; all are disguised. None of the following letters is designed to be copied or to be treated as a model to be followed. They are meant to be seen, as are all the letters in this book despite some of the unlikely writers and recipients, as examples of real letters between real people.

1. Setting up meetings

Letter to a colleague of some five years ago.

Dear Susie

It must be three years since we last met and over five since we worked together. Now you've looked at the bottom of the page at least part of the mystery is over.

One of my spies, John Frencham to be precise, assures me you are still with Computalot, not only having survived its various redundancy and merger adventures but also getting promoted more than once to boot. Congratulations!

The reason I am writing is to ask an enormous favour of you. I want to pick your brains on the subject of satellite communications. I know that you moved out of that when Pinchers & Whizkids bought up your European division and may not feel you are 'up-to-date'; I also know your knowledge is much greater than mine.

The reason for all this is that I am intending to move out of telecoms (I am still with AD Ltd) as I am convinced my future here is going to be slow and boring. I should make it quite clear that I am not expecting you to know of any job opportunities anywhere, but I would be really grateful for half an hour with you.

I enclose a CV, which will give you some of my recent background, and I will telephone in the next few days to see if we can find convenient time to meet.

Yours,

Pam (Forrest)

Encl.

Observations

A reasonably chatty yet businesslike letter. Introductory paragraph followed by recognition of Susie's progress. Then – what Pam wants and why. Note also the clear disclaimer in paragraph 4. Also, no blah about catching up on social gossip. They were seemingly good colleagues rather than bosom pals! We do not know from the letter what kinds of roles Pam and Susie have. It does not matter – they do!

An e-mail version of the above might look like this.

Job Search Job search!

Hi Susie

Time flies, must be 3 yrs since we met. I'm on the move I hope. Getting stifled and feeling stuck at AD. I've decided to try my luck in satellite coms and would really like to pick your brains.

I know you'll say you're out of date since Pinchers & W bought up your European arm, but it's virgin territory for me! I'd love half-an-hour with you.

I've attached my cv, which you might like to glance at; **I'm not expecting any job leads from you, by the way.** It's **information** I need.

I'll phone to see if we can find a good date. If you have time perhaps you could e-mail me some options. Obviously I'd come to you.

Pam

Ps John (F) says you've moved up a couple of rungs. Well done!

Observations

As with the letter the relationship is such that the assumption can be made that the proposed meeting will be acceptable to Susie. The use of bold in the important disclaiming statement seems a good idea with e-mail - often swiftly read. You might also use it in a letter for specially needed emphasis.

Letter to a person referred by someone met recently in a networking meeting.

Graham Armitage
Managing Director
Workcare International
Filtrum Street
Dorking
Surrey   9th September 200X

Dear Mr Armitage,

Your name was given to me by Richard Todd, whom I met recently, and who worked in your organisation for many years as a volunteer. He said that he was sure you would be willing to give me half-an-hour of your time to share with me some of your considerable experience of the charitable sector. Richard also told me that you are extremely busy, but if you *can* spare me some time it does not matter to me how many weeks into the future we go.

My current position as General Manager of a medium sized distribution company will end shortly following acquisition by a major European group. I have spent 20 years in marketing, distribution of various kinds, and general management. In addition I have always done a small amount of local fundraising work.

Now I should like to see if I can use my marketing and management abilities and skills in a full-time paid job in the not-for-profit sector. I am especially interested in overseas aid work and speak good Spanish and Portuguese.

I am not expecting that there would be any opening for me in Workcare International, or indeed that you would know of potential positions anywhere else, but I would like to pick your brains, especially about the complexities of working with foreign governments.

I enclose a brief CV to give you some background information and I will telephone you to see if we can arrange a meeting some time.

Yours sincerely

Michael Tapplehoy

Encl.

Observations

No assumption here about certainty of meeting, despite Richard's virtual promise. This actually scores twice: a) Richard's implied compliment about GA's generosity with rare spare time is faithfully reported b) Michael is properly unwilling to 'take advantage' of it. In addition to including all the necessary elements Michael has set up an implied agenda for the eventual meeting; Marketing & General Management, International Aid involving South America/Africa/Europe?

Letter to a referred person. Writer still very unfocused.

Dear Ms Bushelby

Jonathen Llewellen-Meinhoff-Jones was kind enough to give me your name as someone in a good position to be able to tell me about the NHS with and for which I understand you have worked for over 30 years. He suggested it might be a suitable area for me to work.

He thought that with your management experience in both hospitals and primary care, and recent years in Management Consultancy, you could give me an unrivalled overview of the sort of people who are needed and who succeed and fulfil themselves in the NHS.

I have heard a few horror stories about management in the NHS, which have not particularly surprised me and I share all the aspirations to improve it, which I accept are far in the future, if indeed reachable.

[Frankly I am still searching for career direction, having worked initially in catering then in retail (food). I now have a well-paid job running a major store with Nails & Fencer, but no prospect of further advancement in sight, even if I wanted it.]

I should therefore really appreciate a meeting with you, about half-an-hour if you could manage it, to help me make a judgement about whether to investigate further.

I am not expecting that you would know of any job opportunities for me. I am aware that almost all positions are advertised in the press and NHS Journal. I enclose my current CV, which would doubtless need amending if I were to pursue a career in the NHS and will telephone you in the next few days to see if we can meet.

Yours sincerely

Angela Wellbread

Observations

A full and frank letter. The paragraph which I have bracketed would be much better omitted; it adds nothing positive for Ms Bushelby, and a touch of desperation to the letter. The following short paragraph could also be omitted if 'for about half-an-hour' is just added to the end of the letter. That Angela is unclear about her career direction is evident from her first and last paragraphs. The reference in the last paragraph but one to helping Angela make a judgement might alarm Ms Bushelby. The personal views on the NHS expressed in paragraph 3 are widely held and 'safe'.

2. Thank you letters

Thank you after a network/information meeting.

John Wayne
Six Guns
Four Winds County
Dodge City
Ruislip NW45 1MN   December 12th 200X

Dear John

Thank you so much for your time yesterday. It was really useful to have not only your detailed knowledge of current weaponry laid out so clearly, but also invaluable to hear so much of the history of Colt 45s in particular. I could not have gleaned that from anyone else, and it has helped me to define my aim more closely.

I shall be following up the leads you gave me to Tom Mix and Roy Rogers. In due course I'll let you know how it all pans out.

Many thanks again

Quentin Crisp

Observations
Nice straightforward letter; three 'thank you's', a result, and a promise that does not sound too burdensome on either party.

E-mail thank you letter.

Michael
Yesterday's session was really helpful; I can see now how I could use my past research experience in a local govt. context. Thanks also for the Quango names. I'll get the names etc. of the Italian market research cos. faxed to you tomorrow.

Yours   Tony (Farelli)

Observations
Thanks for an insight this time, rarely obtainable other than in meetings. Two-way help is in evidence here. It is surprising how often this can crop up as a result of a meeting where you wanted information.

CHAPTER FOUR

The Next Best Way

This chapter dispels the common myths about advertised jobs and shows how to analyse job advertisements and identify their sometimes impenetrable requirements. It also shows how to avoid wasting time and effort on unsuitable jobs and create the most powerful impact. The functions and purposes of job advertisements from the employer's viewpoint are examined, and it shows how to construct a response which stands out from the crowd.

Examples of actual advertisements, application letters and results are given (see pp 72–78).

Responding to advertisements

My clients have told me many things about job advertisements, ranging from 'They seem to want everything and nothing' to 'They always want someone aged 24 with 10 years' experience and an MBA'. These and similar myths lead to 'I always seem to be either over- or under-qualified for the advertised jobs' or 'I don't think half of them are real!'

Believe it or not **advertisements are the employers' next most important line of search.** It costs thousands of pounds to place an advertisement in a quality newspaper, and in addition there will be anything between 15% and 30% on top of the new employee's first year's salary to pay if an agency is instructed to help with the selection. This money is rarely spent idly, is often spent very carefully and sometimes very well.

A good recruitment advertisement contains a number of essential elements:

♦ **Puff.** Some information about the (usually glorious) history, state and prospects of the organisation, whether named or not, and its (magnificent) attitude to its workforce. In other words a combination of how it sees itself and of how it would like to be perceived.

♦ **The job specification.** The functions and tasks which at this stage they wish to tell you about. (The employer is in selling mode here.) This may take the useful form of 4 or 5 bullet points, or be buried in a tangled paragraph.

♦ **The person specification.** The abilities, skills, attitudes and experience the employer is seeking. This may be in form of neat bullet points or mixed up with functions or responsibilities. Sometimes the wish list may look over-ambitious, but employers are entitled to aim high.

◆ **Instructions on how to apply.** Often in very small print or scattered about. Whom to write to, where, by when, what to include, what not to. **Disobey at your peril.**

You need to recognise the recruiter's difficulties. In a small space, amidst hundreds of others, the recruiter's advertisement must stand out and catch the attention of preferably no more than 30–40 people who would do the job well including two or three who would do it superbly. This ideal is rarely reached and ads are often imperfectly written. Hence they may sometimes attract several hundred replies or less than ten, embarrassing on either count. Don't make things worse by reading ads carelessly.

Sometimes there is a political dimension attached to a position, which may affect the wording of the advertisement, and the person who will make the ultimate recruitment decision may not have had full control over the writing of it.

You can do nothing about how the advertisement has been written, but you can and must read it intelligently. This also means that you can only sensibly reply on the basis that the writers mean what they say. So if it says 'Only the super-ambitious need apply' and you are not, don't waste your time. You would either get found out or possibly land a job you would hate.

It can be psychologically extremely damaging to receive frequent, negative responses to job applications. You owe it to yourself to avoid this by rigorously analysing job advertisements and establishing that you can offer an 80–90% match to their requirements, especially to the person specification. Ultimately people buy people.

Remember also that however well written the advertisement, however appropriate the candidates, during the recruitment process the job/person specification will be subtly, sometimes markedly, changed to fit or incorporate some of the specific personal qualities/skills/experience of the best candidates. This is tough if you fitted the original specification exactly, but there is nothing you can do about the other candidates.

Star story

If you really want a job ignore an apparent mismatch with the specification

I had a client, Tony Smith, who provided a perfect example of this and of a couple of other 'non-standard' matters. He had worked for a major life insurance company, with the title of marketing executive. When I first heard it this title sounded rather lowly to me, but it emerged that he had had two marketing managers working for him and he reported to the managing director.

It was simply a quirk of this particular long established company deriving from old hierarchical ranks that moved from supervisor to manager to executive and director. It presented a problem about what title to put on his CV; Marketing Manager would have placed him too low in the eyes of anyone familiar with his old company, Marketing Executive too low in anyone else's eyes. It was resolved by his calling himself Head of Marketing, which he was.

He had found an advertised job that he really fancied with a relatively small life assurance company, which was looking apparently for a marketing development manager. Unfortunately it wasn't paying as much as he wanted, in today's terms about £45k. There seemed to be a further problem in that the age range specified for the job was 28–35. Tony was 46.

Tony, who knew a bit about the company, thought they had pitched the job too low and really needed someone of his experience and expertise, who could achieve more, more quickly.

We decided on a full-scale attack. In his application Tony stated why he thought a bigger job was needed. The recruitment agency interviewed him, mainly as a benchmark for six or so younger candidates who more closely fitted the specification. However the consultant who interviewed him was so impressed that he then persuaded the principal to interview him 'as a wild card', alongside three people who matched the original specification. Tony got the job, or rather he got the one he had specified, a level up, at the equivalent of £60k today.

Scanning

Scan widely across the maximum possible number of relevant publications. Consult *British Rates and Data* (*BRAD*) in your public library for others. *BRAD* has an unrivalled list of UK publications and includes virtually all the daily, weekly and monthly newspapers, leisure/interest and trade magazines in the UK. It gives their circulation and readership figures, and the markets they serve. Many carry job advertisements, sometimes ahead of the national press.

Advertisements for jobs appear in newspapers, trade magazines, professional journals, special interest magazines, subscription-based magazines and even free sheets, as well as on the net. Publications range from international to national, regional and local. That is the problem with advertised jobs. They are there waiting for every Tom, Dick and Harriet to have a go at.

When scanning a newspaper or magazine don't analyse in detail, but mark anything that attracts you and go back to it when you have finished scanning. Pay less attention to job titles than to the small print, where you will find the abilities, skills and experience sought by the advertiser. Sometimes nothing suitable may appear in a given publication for several weeks. Keep scanning; like buses jobs often arrive in threes. I cannot overemphasise the need to look widely, which these days also means rigorous and **frequent** scanning of job sites on the net.

Star story
Interesting jobs sometimes turn up in unlikely seeming places

Some years ago a client of mine, who spoke fluent French and German and who had sales and trading experience in Africa, decided, as a part of his campaign, to write direct to a number of large worldwide trading groups. On his list was the Lonrho Group, which had significant interests in Africa at the time. He had written a good letter to a senior export director which was rapidly put through the Lonrho HR chain of command. Within a week he found himself being interviewed on a short list by the MD of one of Lonrho's smaller subsidiaries for an interesting job based in England 'trading in extract of mimosa' in Africa.

He did not in the end take the job but the point of the story lies in what he learned at the interview, which took place at the time when the executive unemployment problems of the early nineties were reaching their peak. His interviewer told him, 'We advertised the job but we only got 29 replies. It's very hard to find good people out there at the moment.'(!)

They had advertised in *leather*, a respected monthly publication first published in 1867, still selling, and one of the key organs of the leather trade. Extract of mimosa it can now be revealed is or was one of the key ingredients for certain parts of the leather processing business. An advertisement placed in *The Daily Telegraph* at the time would probably have brought in 300 replies including 50 highly suitable ones.

My client had created a piece of luck for himself by writing a speculative letter, he could easily have done it also by looking more widely for advertised jobs.

How to construct your reply

In answering an advertisement you are choosing the most competitive route to finding a job, and it is therefore vital that your reply stands out as excellent.

When you find an ad for a job you think you might like to do you may start to think about how you will apply for it. Each ad requires individual analysis and response. You have one objective at this time – **to get an interview.** To do this you have simply to demonstrate that you are:

- the sort of person they are looking for
- with the skills/abilities/experience they are seeking
- clearly able to do the job well
- keen to do it in this (type of) organisation.

Your CV will not do all of this even if accompanied by a letter exhorting the reader to comb through it assiduously and discover these truths. She or he does not have enough time.

The crucial message you must convey is **how you match their requirements**; you will send your CV, which has probably been requested, but it is your accompanying letter which must deliver this message. How well you do this largely determines your chances of getting an interview, also because the first, sometimes the only, question that the reader of your application requires to be answered at this time is 'Does this applicant match our needs?'

It will probably take you, initially, half an hour to an hour to craft a letter designed to be read in two minutes. But this is the length of time you must be prepared to spend. Success in getting an interview is a function of accurate analysis and good presentation.

> **The aim of your application letter (application forms are dealt with later in this chapter) is to obtain a first interview; all other aims are subsidiary to this. But first you must analyse the advertisement.**

1. **Analyse the requirements** by breaking them down into the elements, which describe the kind of person they are looking for and those which describe job content. Read carefully sections describing the organisation/company. This advertising 'puff' can often be revealing. Within limits, disregard age and salary factors. (Remember Tony Smith in the star story above.)

2. **Underline or highlight the person specification elements** and check where you can claim to match them. If you have less than an 80% match you will probably be wasting your time proceeding any further.

3. **If you match, then go on to underline, preferably with a different colour pen, the job specification.** If you can total 80% for person and job specification combined, which might be 90% of person and 70% of job, it may be worth a

try. There may be others applying who have 100% of both, but their letters may not convey their message adequately. **Yours will.**

4. **To help you make your application stand out as excellent,** consider the job as a whole. Try to visualise it and how it fits in to the organisation. Think what else in the way of abilities, skills and experience not specified in the advertisement could be useful or even vital. List them on a piece of paper as they occur to you, uncritically. Allow up to half-an-hour for this exercise with the first few advertisements. Few other applicants will do this. Any of these extra items could be worth adding in to your letter. You don't need many, one is good, more than three too many. Eliminate from your list those that are simply not relevant to the job in question.

Application letter construction and presentation

Letters should be one or two uncrowded pages, word processed unless handwriting is specifically requested. This is very unusual nowadays but occasionally wanted for graphology analysis. Everything in your letter must be positive. **No apologies**: 'I do not have this but I have something else'. Use of 'but' or 'although' is often a danger sign.

Start with an opening paragraph which names the job title, reference number if applicable, publication, date, etc and a short sentence summarising why you are applying for the job. This paragraph serves to introduce the next element.

A **table** headed:

Your requirements   **My qualifications** (give more lateral space under this heading, you will have more words to fit in)

In the left-hand column quote from the advertisement **the actual words** which relate to the **person specification**. There will be usually some three to six items. Sometimes you can group them, eg 'Good communication and presentation skills'. A table of four to five items is ideal. To achieve this you may need to promote something from the job specification. Sometimes some aspect of the job specification is clearly of much more importance than an item in the person specification. You may wish to promote it to the table. If there is a 'requirement' for which you cannot produce a 'qualification' simply omit it. Its absence may not even be noticed. This is not like networking. Rules often need to be bent or creatively rewritten.

Under **My qualifications** quote brief (two to four lines) achievements which illustrate past use of relevant abilities, experience, etc. These may be extracted from your CV but **do not refer the reader to the CV**, it simply creates work for him/her.

The letter should be designed to make it theoretically unnecessary to read your attached CV. A sifter of some 300 application letters will be grateful to be able quickly to identify your application as suitable for the initial 'Yes' pile.

Job specification. You will often find you have covered most of this with the content of your quoted achievements. Cover the rest of the job specification in one or two paragraphs, quoting relevant experience or ability to do the job based on similar work done in the past.

Concluding paragraphs – your personal impact. Add a brief paragraph to show extra relevant items you can contribute not specified in the advertisement. 'In addition I...' Remember that this can sometimes become the most important part of the letter. If you can produce a really useful extra qualification it can make the difference between being asked to attend an interview or not. Also it can begin the process whereby a role starts to be influenced and shaped to you. The final paragraph should express your enthusiasm for the job and that you are looking forward to discussing it at interview. If you don't get enthusiastic about it, you are unlikely to proceed very far with it anyway.

(For some sample letters and the ads concerned see the end of this chapter.)

When to reply

You should aim to get your letter in as early as possible. It is not unknown for advertisers to close their books after a few days. This has even happened prior to a quoted closing date for applications.

Be careful to follow specific application instructions given in the advertisement. There is one exception, you **may** ignore requests for current or last salary details, unless they come back and make a fuss. If the option is given to telephone or write, try to telephone – you may be able to get valuable additional information about the job. However, you must be prepared for a telephone interview, sometimes used as a kind of coarse sieve. If a telephone number is printed, but you are only invited to write in, call anyway. Why else is it there? It also demonstrates that you are alert.

Star story
Short and very sweet

A client of mine saw in *The Sunday Times* what looked like an ideal job for her with a new subsidiary of a major blue-chip company. The ad gave a telephone number and invited those interested to ring any time for a discussion about the job. My client analysed the job in detail, even drafting an application letter, and telephoned that Sunday afternoon. She was invited for interview on the Monday afternoon (next day), where she learned that the company had closed its books, was invited for second interview on the Friday following and was offered and accepted the job the following week.

There was a good reason for all this speed. This was to be a subsidiary designed to have a free hand to chase novel ideas for new businesses, to be fast on its feet and adaptable. My client showed she could react quickly and intelligently to an unusual situation. Inevitably, perhaps, the corporation lost her and her boss to a new enterprise two and a half years later, but not before having had very good value from her services until then.

Application forms

These are mainly used by public sector and large organisations. Whilst you can usually send your CV in addition to an application form, remember that it may get detached from the form. This is sometimes deliberate, as when so called 'equal opportunities' is applied in reverse, i.e. to deny someone the supposedly unfair advantage of having a well-written CV.

E-mail/website application forms are becoming fashionable also with small organisations. Make sure you follow any instructions given, however annoying.

Complete the form as requested and **do not** fill in boxes with 'please see CV attached'. It only annoys and makes work for the reader. Take full advantage of spaces marked with such phrases as, 'State here how you believe you fit the requirements for the job', 'Additional information to support your application', etc. Use additional sheets when invited to do so.

It is worth taking a copy or two of the form to work out spacing in rough. If not specified, you may type or write (legibly) by hand.

After completing the form you should write a covering letter. A well-designed form, which has enabled you to put across clearly your abilities, skills and experience, may allow a very simple covering letter, which identifies the job title, reference, etc and adds an enthusiastic paragraph, looking forward to the interview.

If the form has not allowed this, you may need to write a covering letter along the lines recommended for replies where no application form is involved.
If past salary details are requested, it is permissible to write in the space provided 'details at interview'. (See Chapter 7 The Negotiation Game.)

After your application

Follow up in two to three weeks if you receive no immediate acknowledgement of your letter to check that your application has arrived and to reaffirm your interest. Acknowledgements from advertisers take time and come in many different forms. The most frequently encountered are:

♦ A card or letter simply stating that your application has been received and is receiving attention and that you will be advised further. (Action – allow a further two to three weeks, or a week beyond any date quoted, before following up again.)

♦ A card or letter stating that if you have not heard further after 'x' weeks, you will not be called for interview on this occasion. (Action – none.)

♦ A letter of a standard variety stating that candidates with attributes/ experience/etc more closely matching their requirements have responded. (Action – none.)

♦ A personal letter from the person you wrote to, or his/her boss, saying nice, specific things about your letter, but unfortunately, etc, etc. (Action – allow sufficient time for the recruitment for this job to be completed, say six to eight weeks, and request a meeting for advice or information, i.e. to create a networking opportunity.)

♦ E-mail equivalents to all the above require the same actions.

Note: Negative replies often do not give reasons for rejection, and requests for clarification rarely, if ever, yield any useful feedback. Press on with the next application.

A word of warning
Sometimes you feel an advertised job could have been tailored for you and you are tempted not to apply for a less interesting post elsewhere. Do not give in to this temptation. At and after an interview, good-looking jobs can appear worse, and less interesting ones much better. Many, if not most, positions are modified in the light of the recruitment process and the candidates who come forward.

Summary

- Ads generally mean what they say – read them carefully.

- The employer looks for a close match with the person and job specification.

- Give evidence in your reply of exactly how you meet the requirements.

- Let your enthusiasm show.

- Visualise the role and add an extra qualification or two.

- Remember that a dull looking job may turn out to be fascinating, and vice versa.

- The aim of your letter is to get an interview – not the job.

Letters fit for the purpose (responding to advertised jobs)

Star story

A breath of fresh air

My client, a woman of around thirty, had recently written her first job application in the recommended way, and as a result had had an interview for the job she had applied for with Cadbury Schweppes. She came back from the first interview with this simple story:

'It went really well and I am pretty confident (*which she normally wasn't*) that I've got a second interview (*she had*). It started by his saying (*'he' was the personnel manager*): "We've had 361 replies to our advertisement for this job, but your letter stood out from all the rest. It was like a breath of fresh air! I didn't even look at your CV. I just said, I want to see this person." ' She was thrilled and rightly so, for, although she never got quite that accolade again, it set her on a trail of incredible success in getting interviews and job offers.

Here is the advertisement and my client's response.

Forecasting Manager
THE FUSION OF NUMERICAL, MARKETING AND COMMERCIAL SKILLS

C£35,000 + car + bonus

In the soft drinks market, forecasting demand for the year ahead is a challenge to tax the most inquisitive and analytical mind. Many factors can affect it – brand promotions, major account and competitor activity, the weather, even the timing of public holidays! The effective management of our fast-moving business however depends on accurate and incisive information to support all our planning processes – production, resourcing, finance – it underpins almost every activity. That's why the role of Forecasting Manager provides a high degree of challenge, stimulation and visibility. It requires analysing information, accounting for variables and presenting conclusions to management with reasoned, persuasive argument. It means being able to work on your own initiative, yet operate within a multi-disciplined arena, to optimise company productivity and profitability by accurately forecasting demand. A high degree of numeracy, pc literacy and knowledge of statistics are essential, preferably supported by a relevant degree. However, more than this, you will need to have an enquiring mind, a logical approach to problem-solving, good interpersonal skills and the ability to respond well to pressure. Your background should include responsibility for planning or forecasting probably in an fmcg company. The rewards include a salary of c£35,000 dependent on experience plus car and profit-related bonus. We believe in developing our people and their abilities, and prospects for career progression within a variety of functions are excellent. Please send your full c.v. in the first instance to:

Martin Canham, Personnel Manager, Coca-Cola & Schweppes Beverages Limited, Charter Place, Vine Street, Uxbridge, Middlesex UB8 1EZ

22 Feltham Close
Kingston-on-Thames
Surrey KT25 6WR

Tel: 01932 560000

Mr Martin Canham
Personnel Manager
Coca-Cola & Schweppes Beverages Ltd
Charter Place
Vine Street
Uxbridge
Middlesex UB8 1EZ

23rd October 1991

Dear Mr Canham,

I am writing to apply for the position of Forecasting Manager advertised in The Sunday Times. I enclose my cv in support of this application.

I match my qualifications to your requirements as follows:

Your Requirements	My Qualifications
High degree of numeracy, pc literacy, and knowledge of statistics.	HNC Business Studies including statistical studies. Fully familiar with Lotus 1-2-3 software.
Enquiring mind, logical approach to problem solving.	Experience in complex project management. Turned Baby Ribena into a profitable product by cost reduction and refocussing of sales effort following analysis of customer profitability.
Good interpersonal skills.	Experienced in dealing with managers in Production, Marketing, Sales, R&D, Distribution and Purchasing.
Ability to respond well to pressure.	Successfully managed soft drinks planning role for three years. Met all deadlines relating to product relaunches and new product launches in Marketing roles.
Ability to work on own initiative.	Initiated and completed all work associated with launch of new Ribena concentrate flavour, as well as relaunch of Baby Ribena.

/cont'd...

Mr Martin Canham
Coca-Cola & Schweppes Beverages Ltd

_____

My experience in Product Management involved regular liaison with all company functions. I have a well developed analytical approach to problem solving, and experience in selling ideas to all levels of management. My most recent role included forecasting of sales volumes.

Additionally the following points are relevant:

• Eleven years' experience in a large FMCG organisation, including six years' experience in soft drinks.

• Formal Marketing qualification: Diploma in Marketing.

I look forward to the opportunity of coming to interview to discuss this forecasting role in greater depth.

Yours sincerely

C J

Encl.

Observations

An excellent letter in every way. She pulled out from the solid text of the advertisement every important point answering each clearly and succinctly. There is no flannel just simple facts. It doesn't matter that the letter goes onto two pages. It is easy to read; people can turn pages.

A few elements are worthy of further highlighting:

'Good interpersonal skills.' Many people find this difficult to address. This straightforward quoting of experience with managers from six departments works really well, and would register powerfully with anyone from Personnel.

The paragraph at the top of page 2 does a really good job in mopping up aspects of the job specification not covered by the 'qualifications' (achievement stories).

Job advertised in press – response requested by e-mail

This next job was advertised by a recruitment company, who also put their telephone and fax numbers on the ad. If a number is printed, ring it! The recruitment representative would not say who the principal was, but dropped some hints and responded well to my fictitious client's suggestion of sending a brief covering note with the CV to 'clarify how my skills and experience match the role'. The client elected to send a **very** brief covering note with a single attachment consisting of the covering letter proper, one page, with two pages of CV.

SALES AND MARKETING DIRECTOR

C£70k + Car + Benefits   North of England

Our client is a dynamic and ambitious food distributor supplying a range of fresh and chilled products to the foodservice sector. Part of a large and diverse group, this respected organisation is embarking upon its next stage of development as it focuses on its strategy to achieve market leadership by organic growth and acquisition. As part of these plans a senior commercial professional is sought to define these innovative growth strategies.

Reporting to the Managing Director, the Sales and Marketing Director will assume full responsibility for the entire commercial function including procurement. As a member of the senior management team, you will provide leadership, strategic direction and hands-on coaching. Whilst exercising rigorous cost and sourcing controls, you will be accountable for the achievement of ambitious sales and margin targets. This will involve developing and implementing commercial strategies that will maximise profitable business development.

You will be able to demonstrate success at a senior commercial level, characterised by the ability to formulate and implement effective commercial strategy within the foodservice marketplace. Of graduate calibre, with around 10 years' commercial experience within the food industry, you will be persuasive, energetic and have the presence to take business to a higher level. You will also need exceptional leadership and commercial skills to fully realise our clients' opportunities and to develop a growing team. This is a unique opportunity to make a real difference within a progressive environment.

To apply, please send your CV preferably by E-mail to Anthony Musson at Quantica Search & Selection, Quantica House, Warhurst Road, Lowlands, Elland, West Yorkshire HX5 9DF. Tel 01422 370022. E-mail: 31am@quantica.co.uk Visit our website: www.quantica.co.uk

Quantica *search & selection*

Here is my fictitious client's reply, sent as requested by e-mail.

Attention of Anthony Musson

Attached please find covering letter and CV in application for Sales and Marketing Director role in northern food distribution company. Daily Telegraph 10/01/0X.

Best regards

Gordon Bennett

SALES AND MARKETING DIRECTOR (North of England Food Company) – Job Application

Below I have matched my skills and experience to the requirements indicated

The overall requirement

'A senior commercial professional to define organic and acquisition growth strategies'

My current position (since 200X) is Marketing Manager (Fresh and Chilled Products) at Biggest Food Company UK Ltd. The leading position of BFC has been achieved through a combination of small scale acquisitions and an aggressive marketing strategy, which I introduced at the beginning of last year and which was followed then by the other divisions.

The specific skill and experience requirements

'graduate calibre with around 10 years' experience within the food industry'

Six years with Freshfoods Ltd followed by four years at BFC. First degree in Economics (BA Cantab) in-house part-time MBA (Freshfoods in association with Sheffield University)

'the ability to formulate and implement effective commercial strategy within the foodservice market'

Renegotiated contracts with all BFC's major suppliers over last 6 mths, reducing overall costs by 2.5%, shortening lead times and reducing dependency on single suppliers.

'persuasive, energetic with the presence to take the business to a higher level'

Persuaded board I should take over acquisition strategy when director in charge fell ill. Carried out three more acquisitions as team leader. Other parties assumed I held board position.

'exceptional leadership to develop a growing team'

Following BFC acquisition strategy rapidly built a strong sales team from disparate groups from four different companies. Led by example, ensuring every sales person had at least one Key Account and had an individual training plan. Developed more proactive approach in marketing team.

'to make a real difference within a progressive environment'

My early experience at Freshfoods has given me a thorough grounding in all aspects of fresh food purchasing. At BFC I have met or bettered all revenue and profit targets in the last three years and have developed sophisticated incentive systems for suppliers and sales personnel. I would relish the opportunity to take responsibility for an entire commercial function and grow a medium sized operation into a profitable market leader, which I believe I am fully capable of doing.

Gordon Bennett *(CV follows, as does snail mail version of above)*

Observations

This works quite well. Certainly better from the recruiter's angle than wading through a 'full CV' and trying to see how appropriate the candidate is. The invention of 'The overall requirement' also works. It is worth looking carefully for a summarising phrase, either for the job or for the person. The overall tone is assertive and crisp and feels right for the role. NB: belt and braces approach using snail mail is sensible.

Using the information in the ad

Here is the ad.

Valpak

Valpak is the leader in its field, providing a comprehensive range of specialist services to many household name companies. As part of a major expansion programme, we have established a brand new office in the rural setting of Stratford upon Avon. This has created a number of exciting opportunities for talented individuals. The successful applicants will be responsible for contributing and shaping this fast growing company as it undergoes significant change and growth to meet the demands and requirements of its rapidly expanding market.

Technical Development Manager
Basic 40-50k.,car, performance related pay

We require a technically qualified and experienced engineer to lead technical research and project development activities in close contact with equipment suppliers, operating contractors and the public sector.

You will be able to demonstrate suitable experience gained from operations, process engineering or equipment design background as well as the vision to develop and implement innovative and cost effective technical solutions. You must also be able to demonstrate your ability to work as part of a team internally as well as with other organisations.

Key Skills
5–10 years industry experience
Material handling and sorting expertise
Project concept development
Technical understanding of underlying principles
Self-starter
Proven leader

If you are interested in this position please send in a CV together with your current salary details, preferably by e-mail, to our retained consultant, Jonathan Hale, at the address below. Closing date for applications is Thursday 31st January. For a confidential discussion about the position and how you can add value to Valpak feel free to call. Any applications made direct to Valpak will be forwarded on to Evergreen Resources.

Evergreen Resources
The Barn, Bartons Lane, Old Basing, Hampshire, RG24 8AE
Tel: 01256 314620. Fax. 01256 314629, e-mail admin@evergreen.org.uk

It is not well known that Brunel was one of my clients. Here is Isambard's response, by letter rather than e-mail – as agreed following the offered telephone conversation.

Jonathan Hale
Evergreen Resources
The Barn, Bartons Lane
Basing, Hants
RG24 8AE

10 Railway Cuttings
East Cheam
Surrey

12th January 2002

Dear Jonathan
Ref. Technical Development Manager, Valpak, Daily Telegraph 10/01/02

Following our telephone conversation yesterday, which I found most interesting, here is my formal application demonstrating how I match the requirements of the role.

Your requirements	My qualifications
Suitable experience from operations, process engineering or equipment design background.	10 years in process engineering for WT Group and 5 years in packaging equipment design and development with the Mardon Group, including bottling plants and composite materials handling plant.
The vision to develop and implement innovative and cost effective technical solutions.	Conceived and led the introduction of shrinkwrap for pallet packaging of reams. An industry 'first', saving 30% in packaging costs across the WT group.
Ability to work as part of a team internally as well as with other organisations.	Played leading role in marketing committee, which met objective (from MD) to halve packaging complaints in 6 mths. Member of international standards group, which set a commercial standard later adopted by ISO.

Following my BSc degree (2.1) in Electromechanical Engineering I have spent 15 years in process and packaging and in the last 5 years have led a number of research projects including one for a major pharmaceutical supplier to the NHS which led to a £20m contract for my current company. I have worked closely with a number of materials handling equipment suppliers to improve performance and reliability.

As well as a thorough technical knowledge of packaging and packaging services I would bring to Valpak strong IT modelling skills and the ability to take the initiative and to innovate. I recently set up a monthly 'Technical Forum', for in-house technical training of sales people and senior management, which has proved so popular that it now operates fortnightly.

The Valpak expansion programme you outlined sounds very exciting and I look forward to discussing it further, and what I might contribute to it, at interview. I enclose my CV for further information.

Yours

Isambard Kingdom Brunel

Observations

This application letter really set Brunel on his path. It just squeezes onto one page, which is ideal, although two pages are acceptable if needed to cover the points. The telephone conversation (a must if offered) allowed him to write 'Dear Jonathan' with confidence, demonstrating his bridge building skills, and to cut the preamble to nothing. He could have listed the key skills mentioned in the ad, but all are covered either under 'My qualifications' or elsewhere in the letter. The extra items in the penultimate paragraph look very useful.

CHAPTER FIVE

Helping Others to Help You

This chapter covers unsolicited approaches to recruitment consultants and speculative letters direct to organisations. It explains what their reasonable requirements and interests are and how to meet them. It also stresses the absolute need in **this** context of being focused on what you are looking for and what you can offer and on how to put this across clearly and attractively. You will learn how to get meetings and start to build relationships.

The chapter gives a variety of examples of actual and invented letters including an unsolicited approach by the author and its results, which include indirectly this book.

Approaches to recruitment agencies and direct to employers

The chapter heading should be your aim with all aspects of your career move. You need to provide this kind of help in all directions. Sadly there are a number of people who believe in shortcuts to finding the right career move. They argue that **their** background and/or qualifications equip them ideally for a career move into this or that kind of organisation. Or they may believe they have a very good CV and that any employer or recruitment consultant who read it properly would want to employ or place him or her immediately. Instead of all this 'difficult networking business' why not dash off a lot of letters and get meetings that way? They tend then to complain about the lack of interest shown in them by employers and recruitment agencies.

The problem is that these hoped for employers or 'placers' are busy with other things, like running their organisations or looking for specific people for specific jobs.

Placing in the sense of agencies finding a job to fit you simply does not happen, other than when an Internet site matches your details electronically against job specifications and occasionally finds a rough match. However, recruitment consultants do have jobs to fill, and it is also possible to find the right career move initially by writing a motivating letter direct to an employer.

For both these routes you need to have a **very** clear focus on the kind of role you want to play in what sort of organisation.

Search and selection/recruitment agencies

There is a myth that such agencies are supposed to help you. This however is not their function. They work for and with employers, who pay them for their services. You are their stock in trade and, just like any other stock item, if you don't have a label, or your packaging is damaged or of poor quality, you will tend to get left at the back of the shelf.

The analogy holds for a piece of merchandise with a clear label and of known provenance and quality. For such a job seeker an agent is often prepared to invest time and effort to secure the proper price and a happy customer, i.e. the employer.

Label is the key word, and **you** must supply it. Recruitment consultants are not career advisers, though they may on occasion give good advice. Before you make any serious approach to recruitment agencies you **must** have a clear idea of career direction, what sort of salary you are looking for, and you must be able to demonstrate that you understand the sector you are aiming in. **You must help them to help you.**

Good specialist consultants know their markets/industries/sectors often better than many of the people working in them. They are very useful connections for job seekers, and they **do** have jobs.

Agencies work in a variety of ways and at every level from junior clerk to top international CEO. Your job is to **search** for those appropriate to your aspirations and **select** the most suitable for your needs. That is, after all, what the agencies do.

Some advertise all jobs and filter or **select** from responses, passing on the best seeming ones to the principal. They may additionally carry out preliminary interviews and pass on long or short lists of favoured candidates to the principal. They are paid to be choosy.

Others only **search** using their own contacts, research assistants and 'stringers', and/or using databases of various kinds. Many agencies both search and select; all of them like well-packaged goods with a clear label, a clear purpose, and a short CV.

A few headhunters actively promote talented job seekers, but no agency will be of much use to you unless you get to see them face to face. This is easy enough if you come to their attention when they are in the process of looking for someone like you, but a lot more difficult when they are doing other things.

How to approach agencies

1. Consult *The Executive Grapevine*, a commercial publication listing hundreds of recruitment agencies, and the Federation of Recruitment and Executive Search (the trade association), newspapers, journals, etc to make lists of relevant companies. Scour the net.

2. Create a brief, preferably one-page CV (see Chapter 2). At the bottom write FULL CV AVAILABLE ON REQUEST. If you have a two-pager already and if it has plenty of white space around the text, this may well suffice.

3. Construct two kinds of letter.

◆ For agencies you hope to see, perhaps 5–20 specialists in your field, a brief one-page letter to say:
   – Why you are writing to **this** agency. You might, for example, quote their known specialist status, or mention that they have been recommended by someone or quote some other link. (These things must be true.)
   – What sort of job you are looking for and that you would like to meet with them, whether or not they have any suitable current assignment. You should enclose a brief CV and follow up by telephone two to three days later.

◆ For another maybe 100 + agencies you do not expect to see, a fuller one-page letter to contain:
   – Details of the sort of job you are seeking. You should include a paragraph on abilities, skills and experience. You can add one or **a maximum** of two major achievements with no more than three lines for each.

- Paragraph(s) to cover CV enclosure and acknowledgement that you do not **expect** them to see you, **or even to reply to your letter,** but would of course be available for an 'exploratory meeting', and would be grateful if they would add your details to their database.

Do not follow up for at least a month, and ask then if they have your details readily accessible, give them some news about your job search, ask about the market in general terms. The objective of this is to begin to build a relationship. But you should keep the conversation very short unless of course the other party prolongs it.

> **The more agencies who have your details, the higher your chances of finding a job through this route.**

Keep in touch with those you get to see and follow up by telephone after a month or so any individual who is courteous enough to reply to your letter.

Remember!

- Recruitment consultants' best filing systems are often in their own heads.
- The best way to get to see a consultant or headhunter is to be referred by someone in your contact network who has used the agency at some time.

Do not be discouraged by apparent lack of interest from agencies. They are quite properly disinterested in you personally, and they do have jobs to do as well as, potentially, a job for you.

(For examples of letters to agencies see pp 88–89 at the end of this chapter.)

Direct approaches to organisations

There is no reason why anyone has to reply to an unsolicited letter. Companies and organisations often behave just like people. Think when you last responded to an unsolicited letter and invited a stranger to call at your house. You may never have done so but if you did you will have had a very good reason. **The unknown writer was almost certainly offering something you were interested in hearing about/looking at.** It is exactly what a direct approach must do.

Your letter must motivate the reader to want to see you, not to give you a job. What you want is the chance to earn a job offer later. Opportunities to write motivating letters often arise in the course of networking. You will meet people, who mention particular organisations that might need your talents, but who cannot introduce you to a further useful networking contact in that organisation. It may be an organisation that is actually expanding in an area where your strengths might be useful or it may be one, which just seems to be the right kind of organisation for you.

At this point you might write to a senior employee in an appropriate position. You must offer specific skills and a defined potential benefit or role. The purpose of your letter, however, is to get a meeting not a job. If your offer is unclear your letter will, quite correctly, end up in the waste bin.

A specific role need not necessarily exist. If you have done your homework you may be able to create a completely new job, which the organisation had not realised it needed.

Individually targeted letters

Ideally one-offs, they can be modified from a basic standard letter in many cases. While you must know what you have to offer organisations to which you write you may not know what job titles are appropriate or where in a complex organisation you might best be employed. However, top managers and CEOs are always on the look out for good people to employ (**either now or in the future**) and will take time to see interesting looking people, who convey clearly what they can do.

Letter structure and content (one page only)

You are writing to a particular organisation because you want to work for it. You should write to the CEO, MD or head of discipline, eg sales director, someone preferably two levels of management above your hoped for level. The reason for going two levels up is simply to get to a level where the viewpoint may be wider. Do not write to HR/personnel (unless that is the area in which you want to work). They are frequently the last part of the organisation to hear of a need for new people to be employed. This may sound odd but is logical. Most employment needs are defined within the relevant department and it is often only when sales or accounts department has tried and **failed** to recruit someone that they ask for help from HR/personnel.

The letter

Draft an opening paragraph referring to what you believe the company does, and does well, to its style and reputation – a moderately flattering pen picture, especially of those aspects that interest you. **NB Later you will throw away this paragraph in its entirety.** (Flattery gets you nowhere, and the person you are writing to will know much more about it, usually, than you.) You write it to provide yourself with a focus for the rest of the letter.

The real letter then starts with what you have to offer: abilities, skills and experience and where you think you can make a contribution to the organisation you have just described. You may also include, or alternatively start with, a relevant **and** impressive achievement story. This opening paragraph should aim to grab the reader's attention and ensure that he/she reads on. You might refer to some current events, which affect the organisation, or to something which you read about it in the press. Remember to focus on benefits you can provide, eg increasing sales, or decreasing costs, specialist skills and knowledge, whatever you have to offer.

Subsequent paragraphs might offer brief concrete evidence of your key strengths in action (one or two achievements) and the suggestion that you have an **exploratory** meeting to discuss how you could help them **either now or in the future.**

The purpose of a speculative letter is to get a meeting with a potential employer. It is a specific offer of your expertise to an organisation. If you send out enough of them, a few may arrive at a time when someone is actively considering advertising a job, but has not yet done so, or when expansion plans are under discussion for which additional staff may be needed. However, your letter could arrive two to three months before such a time, so it is important that the meeting you request will address a potential job **either now or in the future.**

Last paragraph

Motivating/speculative letters are no substitute for networking. They work only when the writer is reasonably well focused, and they work best when real enthusiasm for the target organisation is evident in the letter. Remember too that they **have worked** whenever they produce a **meeting.** They are also very difficult to write. You will usually do better if you get some help and listen carefully to any constructive/critical comments.

Mass mailings

Mailing a large number of identical letters can only be considered if you are very clearly focused on finding a well-defined type of job, eg sales management in FMCG or pharmaceuticals, cost accountant or financial controller, Java programmer, production management in food processing, etc.

In all cases your CV **may** be included, preferably a brief one, provided that it supports your letter entirely and contains no distracting information. In most cases however the CV is itself a distraction from the letter.

Follow up

Individual letters or restricted mailings should normally be followed up by a telephone call within two to three days. (Mass mailings will take too much time.) Be prepared to be brushed off or ignored; you have after all sent an unsolicited letter, which may quite properly be consigned to the bin.

> **Mark your letter Personal, or Private and Confidential.**

(Examples of motivating letters (pp 90–92) follow letters to recruitment agencies (pp 88–89) at the end of this chapter.)

Summary

Agencies

◆ Appreciate who recruiters work for and what they need.

◆ It's a numbers game – expect to be ignored and rejected.

Direct approaches

◆ Do not approach until you are clear about what you seek/what you have to offer.

◆ Your immediate objective is a meeting – not a job.

Letters fit for the purpose (to recruitment agencies)

Ivor Rollfew Esq.
Finde, Pollish & Flogg
No.1 St James' Arcade
London W1 1AA

15th September 200X

Dear Mr Rollfew

Sir Bentley Rover, whom I met recently at his Mayfair offices, gave your name to me as one of the best search consultants operating in the retail sector.

I am currently hoping to make a career move within that sector, having just six months to go before my 3 year contract with Platinum Retail comes to an end. In that time frame I shall have seen through the recent store expansion scheme and the associated merger with the Silverwares Group.

My retail career spans 15 years. After completing an MBA at Oxford Brookes I worked for Muckyshops, the giant High Street chain. Since then I spent four years with the Middle England Department Stores Group, first as Merchandising Director then as Operations Director before joining Platinum.

My strengths lie in a capacity to grasp nettles, which others have left growing, allowing me to increase operational profits at Middle England by 45% over two years, and the ability to develop and articulate a clear strategic vision for growth and profit, a legacy which I shall leave for Platinum. My overall track record speaks for itself (I enclose a brief one page CV).

Ideally I am looking for a Managing Director or CEO position, depending on the size and complexity of the operation. I am currently earning £90k plus bonus and package worth approximately £30k. I would hope in my next role to improve earnings substantially.

I will call later this week to see if we can meet for a talk in the not too distant future, though I appreciate you may have no suitable current assignment.

Yours sincerely

Colin Cable

Observations

Simple straightforwardly flattering opening, though note that it was Sir Bentley not Colin doing the flattering – Colin merely reports it. This is the kind of letter consultants love to receive. It is crystal clear, and sooner or later the consultant will want to see Colin to discuss a role that will fit him well. Mr Rollfew, like most headhunters, wants to know salary details. Colin has shown what he can command but given nothing away which could limit his negotiating power. We do not have any idea how old he is either. But he sounds good on paper! You must be focused when you write to headhunters. And, have a short CV!

Lars Tope
IT Executive Selection and Discreet Search Ltd
Neasden Towers
Cricklewood
London N40 4TI

3rd December 200X

Dear Lars

You will probably not remember me. We did meet however about 4 years ago when you were working for Finde and Flogg. You put me forward for a very interesting IT job with The Plastic Bucket Company, where I was just pipped at the final interview by a candidate with rather more relevant experience than I could muster.

I am currently with The Wooden Nickel Corporation, as Head of IT Service Development, who invited me to join them to help with all the IT changes associated with their changeover to plastics. That job is now complete and I am looking for more challenge than my company can be expected to provide.

I believe my next role should be that of IT Manager. I have a team here of about 25 just on development projects and deputise regularly for the IT Director. The role I want would probably be with a smaller organisation concerned, for preference, with providing services rather than goods (50% of Wooden Nickel sales come from consultancy services of different kinds).

Fortunately my employers went for my recommendations for state-of-the-art systems, so I am up-to-date technically. However I know that my greatest abilities are in team leading and motivating, and in working with non-IT management to find ways of improving business practices using appropriate IT support systems.

I enclose a brief CV and a separate sheet detailing my specific IT skills and experience, and I would be grateful if you would put me on your database.

There is no need to reply to this letter, but I will give you a ring shortly to see if we might meet sometime and to check if you need any more information.

Best regards

Roger Bacon

Observations

*However brief your previous contact with an agency has been, and if only by letter or telephone, it is worth quoting. The opening sentence is unnecessarily negative. He **could** have started: You may remember we met four years ago when... Also whilst coming second is OK it is unnecessary to add detail about lack of experience. You might expect e-mail only for IT job search, but letters still work in all areas.*

Letters fit for the purpose (motivating letters to organisations)

This is the hardest kind of letter to write in job search. You are, in a way, writing into the void. There is no advertisement to get your teeth into; there is no familiar person whom you can cite to help you in your cause. So you really must acquire the maximum data you can get about the organisation and, if possible, the person to whom you are writing. At the same time you will use a minimum of all this information in the final letter, which must of course be brief.

Here are two real letters that worked extraordinarily well, and a fictitious one that looks as though it would work. In each case the writer demonstrates **the vital element of clear focus.** The first is the letter that got the meeting that led to my first career counselling job.

U R A Neymyno Esq
Career Counselling Firm No1
1 West End Street
London WC1 1AA

January 1990

Dear Mr Neymyno

Your organisation has been recommended to me as one of the leading career and outplacement consultancies operating in London. I am writing to propose a brief meeting to discuss the possibility of my working with you either now or at some time in the future. I fully appreciate that you may currently have no vacancies but would be very grateful for half an hour of your time.

I have twice in my career benefited from professional career advice and believe I have the necessary skills and abilities to help other professionals and managers to determine career direction and achieve their career goals.

My background has been in marketing, with Wiggins Teape and Appleton Papers Inc and in general management with the Lawson Mardon (packaging) Group. I have considerable experience in running training seminars for small groups, mainly with the WT Group, as well over 10 years' listening experience as a Samaritan volunteer. I have well developed analytical skills and a creative approach to finding solutions to difficulties of all kinds.

I enclose a brief CV to give a broader picture of my experience and will telephone in the next few days to see when we might meet.

Yours sincerely

Graham Green   Encl.

Observations

Remarkably this letter, of which I sent out 22 copies in three batches, yielded 13 initial meetings, from which 6 vacancies emerged. Two of these I was not considered for further, two positions were offered, one of which I accepted, and two arose approximately six months later, by which time I was happily settled in the job I had accepted with Chusid Lander. I do not think it is an especially good letter but it went out to a traditionally open industry at a time when career counselling was in an expanding phase, and it did mention some key elements: listening, analytical skills, positive experience on the receiving end. *My background looked respectable, the CV revealed public school and Oxbridge, all of which would have helped in the industry at that time.*

This next letter was sent to architectural practices. The author, a painfully shy and introverted man, was an unqualified accountant, aged 59, who had found networking next to impossible. He was helped considerably by his Career Counsellor, Roy Blair, one of my early mentors at Chusid Lander – only the address is phoney.

Eesoh, Terric & Leening
Southend Pier
Essex

February 1991

Dear Mr Eesoh

You recognise keenly, I know, the need both to keep tight control on finance and to delegate administrative functions with the confidence that enables partners to concentrate on their areas of specialised expertise without niggling worries and distractions.

This factor can dramatically multiply the efficiency and so the perceived image of a partnership.

If internal harmony is to be maintained and developed, however, the administrator must fit in as a professional among professionals, and be one who recognises his role and responsibilities while remaining always aware of the line drawn between his function and that for which the partnership is in being.

I have spent my working life in comparable environments and could bring accountancy, planning and organisational skills to bear while 'fitting in' as a member of your team.

Could we meet for a brief exploratory discussion of my usefulness to your organisation? I could make myself available at most times to fit into your busy schedule.

Sincerely,

B....J....

Observations

It is a clever letter for a number of reasons. 1991 was a time when many architects did their own administration, the partners often taking on the job in turn. The writer puts himself firmly in a subordinate position, he knows his place. Architects generally hate administration; this letter offers an end to all that. Also there are one or two masterly phrases:

'enabling partners to concentrate...without niggling worries and distractions.' *This really hits the spot.*

'I have spent my working life in comparable environments.' *As Roy used to point out with glee a meaningless phrase, insofar as anything can be compared with anything else, but which conveys somehow total familiarity with architectural practices (the writer had none).*

There are other almost subliminal subtleties. The partners are invited to **'delegate with confidence'** *and assured of the writer's* **'usefulness'** *to them.*

'Exploratory' *and* **'either now or in the future'** *are good standby phrases for regular use in motivating letters.*

The letter was sent without any accompanying CV (it was not a powerful one) to 32 practices. There followed 9 job meetings and two job offers, one of which was accepted.

The next letter is invented to illustrate some basic principles. The writer here has a clear objective in the sense that he wants to use his administrative and organising skills as a stabilising force within a commercial company with a fast-moving and busy culture. He is writing to a select few medium-sized marketing/design/image consultancies that he believes will be interested in his background and knowledge.

Ms Leader
Chief Executive
Premier League Ltd
Regent Street
London W1 1AZ

1st March 200X

Dear Ms Leader

[Your organisation is renowned for its success with public sector work in particular for a number of image-raising successes, including recently the CAB and the COI. I am also aware of the involvement of your company with one of the major train operating franchises and your recent success in completely rehabilitating the share price of one of the leading oil companies in the UK.] *This is the paragraph you don't send. Replace with a simple heading. Say:*

Public sector developments
I believe that under this government there will be a number of changes, particularly in the Health Service but also in other sectors, requiring important changes in public perception which will need the injection of commercial impetus and marketing expertise that can only be provided by organisations like Premier League.

For the last three years I have been Deputy Chair of an NHS national project committee focused on public/private sharing of certain key facilities. Our report will be published next week.

Although recently there have been signs of the return of some passion to the NHS, frankly I have missed the buzz of the private sector. I have 10 years' senior management experience in the NHS, preceded by 10 years spent in advertising, mainly with Old & Rubicon in media buying and traffic. I have not forgotten the importance of meeting client deadlines against the sometimes conflicting artistic and production demands.

I believe that my knowledge, experience and project management skills could be of interest to Premier League, either now or in the future, and would welcome the opportunity of a brief discussion on some specific proposals I have. I will telephone in a few days to see when might be convenient to meet.

Yours sincerely

Art Pressgang

Observations
The opening paragraph is written purely as a focusing device for the rest of the letter, which should probably be sent without an accompanying CV. Art sounds in no hurry to find his next position in the private sector, which always allays fears in the potential employer. I think it would be of some interest to Ms Leader to meet him. Remember that the objective of the letter is to get a meeting, nothing more at this stage.

CHAPTER SIX

Meetings of Minds

This chapter explores extensively what is being or should be being communicated in the job interview. It stresses the two-way nature of what should be considered meetings rather than interviews and the importance of discussing what the interviewer wants to know — that you are ideal for the job. It shows how to promote yourself in a natural, easy fashion, and also covers the practical elements including before, during and after the interview.

You will be shown how to **deal with** questions rather than simply answer them. The chapter also examines a number of favourite interview questions. It analyses a number of different pieces of typical dialogue to expose what is going on.

The psychology of the interview

Being nervous in or before an interview is normal if sometimes frightening. Arguably it is a good thing if it results in being keyed up and alert. What is not good is being upset by the idea of interviews to the extent that you worry about blowing the whole job at the interview stage. On its own interviewing may not be the best way to choose who is the best person for a particular job. However, it is a necessary part of beginning to get to know another person, gaining reassurance, and exploring the degree to which the job, organisation and person are a good fit. A number of independent surveys have shown that interviews are the least effective predictors of suitability for the job, ranking way below assessment days and psychometric testing. However, no one has yet come up with a system for recruiting without an interview.

Some people perform well in interviews, but most employers, unless interviewing or being interviewed is a key part of the role, will not take too much account of interview technique, good or bad. Sadly interviewers' own technique is often lacking. However, bad technique can inhibit or damage the quality of communication in more important areas, and is unlikely to help in any area.

A meeting about a job

This is what an interview is. You have received a letter or a telephone call inviting you to an interview, a meeting to discuss a job. How should you approach it? It is time now to take off the packaging and reveal the quality of the goods. The potential employer wants to measure you against other candidates to find the best person for the role.

Your task is to show the interviewer how well you match the requirements of the job and, ultimately, to obtain the job offer, which you may or may not accept. In most cases, a first interview will be followed by a second, and sometimes by a third, before a job offer is made. Your short-term objective is to get to the next job meeting.

The interviewer wants you to be good

This simple but powerful fact is working for you before every first interview. Until this point the recruitment process has been geared to finding reasons to reject applicants. Now the recruiters want to choose one of the applicants and they would like the best. It is *your* responsibility to demonstrate that *you* are that person.

This is where the **label** is so very useful. The concept of a label was introduced in Chapter 1. In the interview situation an expanded version of your label is precisely the answer to the request, 'Tell me/us a bit about yourself/your career to date.' If by any chance you are not asked this kind of question, you can simply offer the information early on yourself. 'Would it be helpful if I told you a bit about myself?' The offer is never turned down.

Think of your label as a one minute 'commercial'

The content of your 'commercial' should be a mixture of:

◆ your key strengths (those relevant to the job in question)
◆ something about your background
◆ one or two career highlights or achievements and perhaps a phrase which links all this to the job
◆ some personal details (optional).

There is a problem that you have to address. How much detail do you put in? This is early in the interview and you don't know what is preferred. It is therefore good to keep it short, and finish with an offer to 'expand on any area if you wish'.

It should take you some time to prepare a good commercial. It is difficult and you may want to write it down and learn it, but be careful. Here are two examples. Which do you prefer?

Example A

I am married with two children. I would describe myself as a good communicator, especially to small audiences. I have an analytical and creative approach to problem solving and an ability to sell complex ideas at board level.

The early part of my career was spent in the paper industry, where in 15 years I was promoted through a variety of sales and marketing positions and visited most of Western Europe perfecting my French and German.

For the last 5 years I have been working as a consultant in the motorcar manufacturing industry, helping manufacturers to set up more effective marketing channels, especially in Europe but also in the Far East, where I have acquired market knowledge relevant to the demands of this job and conversational Japanese.

I believe that my main achievements have been the creation of strong corporate relationships across international and cultural divides.

Are there any aspects of my career that you would like me to expand upon?

Example B

I've always been a good communicator. It's probably what made me go for languages at university. I speak fluent French and German and a fair bit of Japanese. I've always enjoyed meeting people from other cultures, and I've done a lot of training – small groups mostly.

I think I'm quite creative, good at finding non-standard ways of doing things, but I can think logically as well. One of the best things I did was to broker a very complex trade and channel marketing deal between Ford and Mazda. Both companies are very happy with it.

I suppose my career breaks down into two chunks. 15 years climbing up the international sales and marketing ladder – that was in the paper trade in Europe – invaluable experience. Then 5 years as a marketing consultant to the motor industry – very interesting. And of course I've learned all about the Far East markets in general and how the big corporations function – very relevant to this job. Oh, and I'm married with two children. Is that enough to be going on with or would you like some more detail?

_A_ is how we write. _B_ is how we speak. You should be in speaking mode.

Job interviews are sometimes thought of both by employers and would-be employees as discussions between unequal partners. This idea must be banished from your mind and, if necessary, gently removed from the mind of the interviewer. The situation is one of equal status for both parties; interviews are about two-way communication of **ideas**, **facts** and **feelings**. Without for the moment considering style let's focus on content. If you focus on getting the content right, style will to a considerable degree take care of itself.

◆ **Ideas** in this context refer to thoughts, opinions, questions and ideas about the job, the organisation, the marketplace or sector, yourself and your career, even about the world in general.

◆ **Facts** are the undoubted statements and answers delivered by each party, i.e. whatever is _treated_ as factual, including statements about abilities, skills and experience.

◆ **Feelings,** expressed usually as **attitudes** include a range of matters of great importance to both parties: indifference, enthusiasm, curiosity, optimism, confidence, doubt, openness, etc. The following typical discussion could be analysed as indicated in the bracketed sections. To some extent consciously or unconsciously it will be.

Interviewer: What we have in mind for this new product manager role is that whoever fills it should act as a catalyst to other departments *(idea)* although it will be firmly based in marketing department *(fact)*. What do you feel about that? *(attitude request)*.

You: That sounds like a sensible and practical approach *(positive and accepting attitude)*. Where exactly does the role fit within marketing? *(factual query)*.

Interviewer: We see it as reporting directly to me as director of sales and marketing *(fact or perhaps idea?)* and sitting alongside the marketing manager and the sales manager, who incidentally are very happy about the idea *(fact?)*. They both need to reduce their workload *(fact – or attitude of disapproval?)*.

You: I think that could be a very workable structure *(attitude of approval)*, and working as a team with them *(idea)* would give the role the right kind of clout with other departments *(enthusiastic attitude)*. You indicated the role would be catalytic *(idea)* which I think I understand in the context of the overall company structure *(explained facts earlier in interview)* but at what level are new product developments sanctioned and launches agreed? *(more facts needed)*.

The above scenario may consist of exactly the **attitudes**, **ideas** and **facts** ascribed to them, but if you were the 'You' above you should get to meet your potential peers as soon as possible, preferably today, to establish **their** attitudes.

It is these things, which are of fundamental importance in establishing a match of person to job. Any or all of them can be hidden or revealed though the last group, **feelings**, which insofar as they represent character traits can be difficult to disguise. Which of them are the most important is your task to establish in the course of the interview.

If your CV and accompanying letter or application form have already expressed your ideas and feelings about the job and the key facts about you, the interview will be that much easier.

Before any interview you should consider the following:

- They must have judged me a likely contender, able to do the job.

- The employers hope the interview will prove them right.

- What interests them most about me is what I can do for them.

- What do I need to find out about this job and these people?

- If there is a good fit I shall try to get an offer/get to the next round.

The interviewer is looking in general for reassurance, and facts are more reassuring to most people than anything else. If there is one key element which employers look for it is interest in and enthusiasm for this particular job in their organisation. Consider therefore how you might answer the (early) question:

Potential boss: What made you apply for this job? (senior new product manager – a middle management, marketing role in a medium to large fmcg group.)

You: I'm very interested in new product development and after some useful experience at Bloggs & Co I feel it is time to develop my career further. I saw the Newways advertisement, and here I am.

or

You: It seems to be just the job I am looking for. I find new product development fascinating. I enjoy the challenge of working with R&D and production, and I would relish the opportunity to build on my experience at Bloggs & Co in an organisation like Newways. What sort of percentage of potential new products do you aim to get to launch stage?

The first implies: 'I'm due a promotion, I've got experience, how about it?'

Interviewer thoughts?
- Minimal interest and enthusiasm.
- Not interested in Newways per se.
- Some self-interest.

The second says: 'I'm keen to move on, I really enjoy this area. This *sounds like* the right job in the right company. Tell me more, please.'

Interviewer thoughts?
- High level of interest and enthusiasm for job.
- Interested in Newways.
- Ambitious and already asking questions. I wonder what the right percentage is?

This interest factor is a vital one, and your interest in a company or job, which has been accepted so far, must now be stated clearly and if possible demonstrated with feeling.

An interview for a job has to become a dialogue or discussion, which explores as fully as possible how well suited candidates and jobs are. Increasingly organisations are employing psychometric testing and or assessment day methods to get to a final short list of two or three, but the final interview remains the final arbiter. Remember that you are ultimately in charge. The offer will come before you have to decide whether to accept it or not.

Staying with content let us look at some of the inevitable topics that you will need to discuss in an interview. These will certainly include your career to date, what you could bring to the recruiting organisation, your CV and your long-term goals. This little list is part of the employer's agenda. You need to know – *how the organisation has developed and what its future might be*. Your research prior to the interview may have revealed some of this, but there is undoubtedly more to be uncovered. If it is an agency interview with a previously unnamed organisation you are starting from scratch anyway. Also you need to know – *how the role relates to rest of the organisation and whether it meets your needs currently and in the longer term.*

What they want to find out

You must accept that your CV will be probed. It is a kind of Aunt Sally that you have put up to be shot at. But unless it contains inconsistencies or yawning gaps, which it should not, the questions you get will be designed to explore, elucidate or confirm impressions gained. Your career to date is of interest insofar as it is relevant positively or negatively to your ability to do this job. What you bring to the recruiting organisation is your particular mix of skills, experience and abilities, which should match the person specification. This is what they want to check out above all. **They want you to tell them that you have everything that they need.**

Another legitimate area of enquiry is that of your goals. At this point it is worth stating that not everyone has clearly defined goals! Whilst to some this is a shocking state of affairs, you must consider, as always, the reason for enquiry. It is simply designed to find out whether your goals match those that the organisation has **with respect to you.** Unless it is otherwise made abundantly clear these goals are always the same. **That you fulfil the role as they see it over the next three years or so, and that you then present them with options to make further use of your services.** If at that point you leave, so be it. If you declare any longer term goals they must be consistent with this and should reflect genuine attitudes. If you are ambitious, by all means say so. If you are convinced that the job has to be tackled in a different fashion from the one they have envisaged in order to make the contribution expected, you should perhaps say so, although not usually at the first interview. You are not expected to be a prophet, and accurate prophecy is very difficult, especially about the future.

What you want to find out

The fundamental question, which you cannot ask, but to which you want an answer, is 'Is this the right job in the right organisation for me?'

Here we will stray slightly from content to style. There is a huge advantage in asking early on in the interview questions of the What. . .? How many. . .? How long. . .? kind about the historical and current development of the organisation and about the numbers of people, things goods/services, etc involved – questions about structure. Why should this be so? Because, outside examination rooms and other forms of torture chamber, they are unthreatening to the person being asked, and the answers given, other than 'I don't know', are in the form of facts or at worst opinion dressed up as fact, which may be treated as fact. Don't forget to ask about your peers. Who are they? How long have they been with the organisation? Will you have a chance to meet them?

Questions concerned with information are usually the easiest to answer. They have the effect of helping the interviewer to relax – she or he may be nervous too. They demonstrate your interest. They help you to work out where the power might lie in relation to the organisation as a whole. Questions concerned overtly with opinion and motivation can be asked later. Remember too that your questions can impress just as much or more than your answers. Just don't get too clever too soon.

It is much more difficult to give prescriptions for style. To an extent you are bound to the style of the interviewer. She or he sets the ground rules for your encounter/meeting/grilling/chat or joust. Your preference should be for a **meeting** at which a discussion takes place between mutually interested parties towards the agreement of a potential contract to the benefit of both parties. For you it is a meeting about a potential career move, and if you demonstrate your interest and enthusiasm by your questions and reassure your interviewer with facts, this is all the style and 'technique' that you will need. So much for the psychology of the interview.

Summary

What an interview is.

◆ It is a meeting about a job
◆ for two-way communication of ideas, facts and feelings

where the interviewer wants you to demonstrate
◆ your ability to do the job
◆ your interest in the organisation

by
◆ reassuring him/her with facts and
◆ showing your enthusiasm for job and organisation.

You need to find out
◆ how the organisation works
◆ what the job and people are like

by
◆ asking intelligent questions and
◆ listening to how your interviewer responds.

Practical matters

Before the interview

First write and confirm the date and time of the meeting, expressing your interest and enthusiasm. The only reasons not to write are if there is simply not enough time for a letter to arrive, or if you are specifically **asked** to e-mail, fax or phone.

Now is the time for research. Preparation for an interview is vital. You need all the information you can get about:

- the organisation/company and its history

- its products/services and markets

- financial performance

- relationships with other organisations

- position in the market, etc.

Sources of information include reference books from your library, your librarian, contacts you have in the organisation, people you have met in the course of networking who may know something about it, the press or trade journals and the organisation itself. If it has a **PR** or marketing department you can ask them to send you information. If the organisation has a website this needs to be fully explored. The Internet will also be an important source of information about the sector, competition, etc.

Check list – before you set off

- **Study your correspondence** to date with the company. If you responded to an advertisement, re-familiarise yourself with its contents. What is it that made them want to see you? Try to find out more about the job and more about the interviewer.

- **Prepare what you are going to say** about yourself and a list of questions, which you will want to put to the interviewer. Work out how long it will take to get to the place of interview. You may wish to make a trial trip first if it is not too far.

- **Dress**: unless you have specific reasons for doing otherwise, you should dress as you would for an important work meeting or marginally more formally, paying particular attention to cleanliness and tidiness.

- **Know exactly where you are going** and be sure to arrive 20 minutes early, giving yourself time to relax and reconnoitre the establishment. Plan to arrive about ten minutes before the appointed time; there are things to be observed in the reception area, posters, notices, copies of trade journals, in-house magazines – and the general atmosphere.

◆ **Take with you**: a folder containing all your requirements for the meeting – spare copies of your CV, correspondence, list of questions and, if applicable, examples of your work; 'open' references, pens and notepad. Leave your briefcase in the car or in reception if you can.

The object of all of this is to look as if you are part of the establishment already. It can only help.

At the interview

This is a meeting about a job for which you must consider yourself a major contender, otherwise you would not have been asked to come. A number of matters should be covered, and if the interviewer does not do his/her job properly you should help him/her.

◆ Description of the organisation, the job and where it fits into the overall purpose and structure, the boss, or bosses, to whom you will be responsible, and the staff you may have reporting to you – also your peers.

◆ Presentation of yourself – your background, abilities, skills, focusing on the particular contribution you can make to the job as described so far.

◆ Questions, from both parties, designed to discover the organisation's needs, style and structure, and to reveal your **competence** and **compatibility**. Competence is usually the first matter to establish and may be the only requirement at a first interview. In due course, compatibility, the 'fit' between you as a person and the personalities and style of the organisation is a vital requirement for it and for you. However, compatibility starts to be assessed, if not formally at least subliminally, from the moment of first meeting – and **first impressions count.**

◆ Terms and conditions and remuneration may also be laid out or discussed. Such subjects should not be raised or discussed by you, as they belong to a later stage – negotiation.

◆ Use open questions. How...? What...? Where...? to elicit information – aim to get your interviewer talking for 60% of the time, 50/50 is ideal.

Frequent or sensitive interview questions

◆ How much do you know about our organisation?
(How interested were you in doing some homework and how effective have you been in ferreting out any useful information?)

◆ What will you bring to our organisation?
(A dream question. List your relevant key abilities, skills and relevant experience, and how you expect these to contribute to the job and organisation.)

◆ Tell us a bit about yourself.
(Another dream question – a chance to give a two minute presentation of yourself. Brief career highlights, key abilities and how it all points to this job as the next logical step.)

◆ What is your greatest weakness?
(You have several choices, but your choice must be true for you. A 'weakness' which comes across as a strength, eg 'can be fussy about (good on) detail', 'impatience with sloppy work'. Or it could be a weakness buried in the past, which you have become aware of and now control. Or it could be denial of any weakness which is relevant to this job. Be careful to avoid flippancy.)

◆ Why was your job made redundant?
  (Straightforward, brief answer needed.)

◆ Do you feel you could have done more in your last job?
  (Were you dynamic enough/too easily satisfied/frightened to 'make waves'? What did you do well?)

◆ Tell us about your worst boss?
  (How good are you at getting on with bosses who are less than perfect? Or what lessons have you learned from a difficult/tough boss?)

Dealing with questions

Questions which you may find awkward, or sensitive, need 'answers' which are *brief*, *positive* and *reassuring*. More precisely put, questions need to be **dealt with** in a brief, positive and reassuring way.

Interviewers do not want to trip up candidates; they want to be reassured about areas of potential doubt. For example, 'Do you think perhaps you are overqualified for this job?' may express a doubt or fear that a candidate might find a job too easy, get bored, and either under-perform or move on. An answer which focuses on challenging, interesting or difficult aspects of the job will reassure the questioner. Questions need to be answered truthfully, but not necessarily with the whole truth, which is often complicated (even misleading) and may be quite irrelevant to a candidate's ability to do the job.

Other questions are often vague or impenetrable. Ask for clarification. If you do not understand a question, say so, and if you do not know the answer admit it. 'They are only easy if you know the answer.'

Hypothetical questions are traps for the unwary. 'If you discovered that sales of one of our range of widgets had dropped to a level which meant that it was no longer profitable, what would you do?' This is not a question you can answer. There are too many possible reasons and remedies. However you can **deal with it** by giving an example of action you took in some 'apparently similar circumstances'. If it turned out well, you can take the credit. If not, you will be able perhaps to show that you learned something. If you can think of no similar situation from your own experience, you can only safely say what information you would need to obtain in order to decide what to do.

Jobs requiring to be filled are sometimes 'Charlie' shaped. In other words vacancies are often modelled on how the previous incumbent, Charlie, performed the role. You do not have to tread in his footsteps. At second or third interview stage it may be very important to explore what the core and the boundaries of the job are and how the organisation can capitalise on **your** particular mix of skills, abilities and experience.

At the end of most interviews you will be asked if you have any further questions. A good last question is: 'Is there any area where you feel I don't meet (fully meet) your requirements?' This can only yield three kinds of answer:

- 'I'm afraid you just don't have the depth of experience we require.'
  (You are merely hearing a little earlier than you would have done by letter that you have reached the end of the line.)

- 'No. I think you match our needs quite well.'
  (This is an excellent thing for them to have said out loud.)

- 'It would have been useful if your research skills had been more extensive.'
  *(**This is a misunderstanding on their part.** Having asked the question you can now correct the situation and maybe get to the next interview after all.)*

Read *Secrets of Successful Interviews* by Dorothy Leeds for a thorough examination of interview questions and how to **deal with them.** You cannot really over-prepare for a job meeting.

After the interview

As soon as possible write a brief report of the meeting, noting things you did well, as well as questions you forgot to put and answers on both sides which were less than satisfactory. Write down the names of any people you may have met and precisely how the meeting finished, i.e. what is to happen next. Keep all this material even if you do not get any further with this job. It may be useful to refer to in connection with another job interview.

If it moves, write it a thank you letter

When you get home write a brief letter to express your interest in or enjoyment of the meeting, your enthusiasm for the job and add anything you wish you had said, which would strengthen your application. Keep it short, half a page is plenty. You should write again in similar vein after second and third meetings, especially when you meet new people. The purpose of this thank you letter is to reinforce your demonstrated ability to meet the employer's needs. Such letters have been known to clinch jobs.

Before you burn your fingers always strike another match

Finally, while going through the exciting and interesting interview process, which may extend into months, do not neglect other aspects of job search and other potential leads, even when they seem much less interesting. This job might appear to be a near certainty, but at any moment, it can be snatched away from you by factors totally outside your control. They may be on the point of offering you the job, when someone, somewhere, issues an edict barring all further recruitment for the next twelve months.

You may go through all the stages of a long recruitment process, only to lose out to an apparently more suitable rival, of whom you know nothing. This situation is much easier to cope with if you have another interview coming up.

Summary

- An interview is a meeting about a job.

- The interviewer is on your side. She or he wants you to be good.

- Consider what is going on in the meeting.

- Reassure with facts and let your enthusiasm show.

- Prepare to ask and be prepared to **deal with** questions.

Letters fit for the purpose

Thank you letter after an interview.

Arthur Karme Esq
Karme Klier & Straite
St Michael's Walk
London W1 1WW

30th December 200X

Dear Arthur

I wanted to say how much I enjoyed our meeting yesterday. I was very pleased also to meet, albeit briefly, Fairley and Justin.

As I mentioned one of the most useful elements I could bring to the partnership is my knowledge of the power industries. We did not pursue this, but I see enormous potential for consultancy and project work for KKS in wind power.

I hope very much to come back for further discussion and to meet the remaining partners.

Yours sincerely

John Gale

Observations
Nicely brief. If John is right about the wind power, he must be in with a chance. Could have been more positive? – **I look forward to the opportunity for further discussion and to meeting...?** *It is early days but they have clearly been 'talking shop' – always a good sign!*

Thank you e-mail

Arthur

Excellent opening discussions – would very much like to talk about wind power opportunities for KKS. Good to meet Fairley and Justin. Hope to come back soon to meet other partners

Regards
John Gale

Ps Attached for interest is non-confidential spec for the Magellan Farm.

Observations
An opportunity seized by John here to move things on, using one of the conveniences of e-mail.

CHAPTER SEVEN

The Negotiation Game

This chapter addresses the necessary question of how much money is going to be spent by the employer to secure the services of you, the employee-to-be. It describes the nature of the 'game' which is played and shows you how to maximise your earnings without jeopardising the job. Theoretical and actual negotiations are illustrated and discussed, demonstrating the importance of the 'want factor', win-win and the power of silence.

Negotiation of salary and package – the 'want factor'

Before negotiation of salary and any accompanying package the scope of the job and its responsibilities should be thoroughly understood by both parties. In particular your contribution must be understood so that your worth can be properly evaluated.

Advertised jobs often mention a figure, eg 'ca £60K', which is technically the start of negotiations. However, you should allow no further discussion of this until you are ready. You are ready when your would-be employer 'wants' you and is at the point of offering the job. Up to that point you have been doing most of the running, selling your abilities, skills and experience against other competing job seekers. The 'want factor' reverses the situation.

Know your bottom line

During the course of the recruitment process most jobs are modified from how they were originally conceived. Good candidates can significantly alter employers' perceptions about how the position fits in to their overall structure. All this may change their view about the value of the job – up or down!

Employers have a duty to keep costs down and therefore to acquire your services for as little as possible. You have a duty to yourself and family. You also have certain basic needs (mortgage repayments, etc) and cannot afford to take a job for less than a certain minimum salary. **This figure must be firmly fixed in your mind before negotiation of remuneration begins.** Employers may have a figure, above which they are not prepared to go – it is less likely to be as firmly fixed as your figure. Exceptions to this are most public sector jobs, or jobs in companies with very rigid job evaluation schemes and/or salary structures. If the employer's maximum is less than your minimum there will be no satisfactory outcome.

Many people, including recruiters, find negotiating salaries or money distasteful or discomforting. Think of it to some extent as a game. If you negotiate properly, it is likely that both sides will feel they have won something.

Negotiate the job before starting on the salary

Employers may often try to strengthen their hand by asking, before the job has been fully discussed, a question such as 'What salary are you looking for?' You should not be drawn by this and should respond along the lines of 'I should be happy to discuss salary if this is the appropriate time. Do you agree that I am right for the job?' Any equivocal answer can be followed up by a suggestion that while you can be flexible about salary, you are more concerned to establish full details of the job and your suitability for it. Perhaps they could expand a little on... (some aspect(s) of the job)? If the employer is not ready to offer you the job, they will usually back off at this point, and the job negotiation can continue. An insistence that they need to know where you are coming from should be met with your insistence that for the right job you are flexible – 'Will I have full responsibility for...?' or 'How quickly will it be possible to implement restructure of the sales department?' – any question about uncertain aspects of the job.

Should the interviewer agree that you are right for the job, you will still want answers as outlined above, but will then want to say something like: 'I want to fit in with your general salary structure. You have certainly a better appreciation of what the job is worth to the organisation. What figure did you have in mind?'

The point is a simple one. Whoever speaks first loses something. Any figure you mention will not be increased and will almost certainly be forced down. Any figure the interviewer mentions represents his proper attempt to buy your services as cheaply as possible and can be pushed up.

Rationally and logically, the employer should make the first offer. They believe you are right for the job, they know what they can afford and the structure of salaries within the organisation. As well as your minimum requirement you must also have in your mind a higher figure – the salary you would like to earn and that you believe to be realistic for an ideal candidate. As a guideline to this you might consider adding 25% to your minimum, or 10% above the 'ca £—' quoted in the advertisement, **whichever is the higher**. Thus, if your nerve fails you and you speak first, this is the figure you will quote, knowing that it will be forced down. You might therefore be surprised, if the interviewer were instantly to accept. No matter, it would clearly be a good deal for both parties.

Win-win and the power of silence

A more likely scenario is that the interviewer will quote a figure near or even below your minimum requirement. **Do not respond immediately.** Remain silent considering your next move. Lost in thought, as you would be if the figure were much higher than this, you must appear disappointed and maintain silence. The interviewer will crack. They want you and it appears that they are off beam; what is more they do not know how far off beam. Eventually, and it may take some time, something will be said. The interviewer will either increase the figure or, more likely, say something like 'Is that not what you were expecting?' or 'You must appreciate that whilst we would like to offer more, blah, blah...'

Your response should be to talk about the job, about the company, how well you feel you would fit in, how enthusiastic you had felt about getting stuck in, etc, and that you had indeed been expecting a higher offer. If nothing is then forthcoming you may come up with your higher figure or 10% above what the company advertised, **whichever is the higher**. You will probably be able to agree on the next figure mentioned or one halfway between theirs and yours.

A typical auction for an advertised job (ca. £60k), for which £55k is your minimum and for which after negotiation £65k is possible, might go as follows:

Interviewer: We would like to offer you the job at a starting salary of £57k plus the package of benefits described which is standard for all our senior executives, and we hope very much that you will accept.

You: (Silent – thinking, bother, now I've got some work to do, and they have pitched it quite well, above my minimum but...)

Interviewer: Well, we said £60k in our advertisement and we believe that this is a more than reasonable offer considering the present economic and market conditions and the benefits package which adds up to some £5k.

You: (Silent for about ten seconds – a long time if you count them. The silence may be interrupted – if not, you say...) I confess I had thought that in view of our discussions and that as well as fully meeting the requirements you specified we agreed that my specific ability to do... would allow... (up to 90 seconds of job talk follows) ... I did think that you would come up with a higher offer?

Interviewer: Well, I appreciate all that but, in view of our current depressed trading figures we do need to watch every penny, but what did you have in mind as a starting salary?

You: In view of the near-perfect match of my abilities and experience to the job I had expected to agree a figure above £60k – of the order of £65 to 70k. (Note: this **means** £65K, but allows them to 'drive a hard bargain' down from £70k.)

Interviewer: I'm afraid £65k was never on the cards, but perhaps we could compromise at £60k?

You: (May either agree or go for £62k, i.e. 13% above your bottom line.)

In this example both parties win. You get more than £55k, they pay less than £65k and even less than £70k. There is an additional advantage in negotiating: the interviewer has a chance to see you working successfully for the first time.

Final agreement

Do not formally accept the offer at the meeting. Say you look forward to the formal offer in writing to which you will then give a written response, say, within 24 hours. The reason for this is straightforward. People occasionally make mistakes or even, more rarely, try things on. The negotiation is complete only when you give your confirmation of the offer. It is best to do this in writing.

Many other tricks may be used by an interviewer either in earlier job meetings or during formal negotiations. Questions such as: 'What were you earning in your last job?' It's none of their business, nor is it relevant to this job in a different organisation. The former is difficult to say politely, but you can at least ask what its relevance is. Ultimately, if pressed, it is probably best to give the figure or a close approximation.

Total shock and horror may be shown when you come up with your higher figure. There is no need to react to this. They are either play-acting or seriously worried. Either way they will move their figure upwards. Remember – **they want you.**

On rare occasions there may be a genuine problem. Their maximum offer does not meet your minimum requirement. Your magic phrase is: 'Would you like to consult?' At this stage you are probably negotiating with your future boss. If they want you they will go to their boss or to the board and squeeze some extra budget from them.

'Package' items

In the unlikely event of your being unable to negotiate the salary upwards, you must negotiate **something.** Season ticket loans, home telephone expenses and/or a salary review after three months, depending perhaps on when the organisation has its annual review. Perks such as pension, life and health insurance, car or expenses are usually standard for all similar positions, though some are related to salary, hence the importance of the highest possible salary.

Bonuses may figure here. So many different schemes are in operation, and most relate to actual salary level, that normally you can only ascertain how the system is designed to work and what levels of bonus have been paid in recent years.

If commissions are payable, they are normally related straightforwardly to job performance or orders received, but sometimes the relationship is complicated. You need to understand exactly what it all means, and what sums have been or are expected to be paid out.

If a car is included in the package it is not recommended that you try to negotiate for a better car. But if you are a car 'buff'...

After the written offer

On receipt of a written job offer you may want to do other things. You may wish to telephone someone with whom you are due to have a second job meeting and get it brought forward. You can say, 'I have had a job offer which I am considering, but I am more interested in the position with your organisation.' **But only if you mean it.** It is important to understand that blackmail does not work in this context. We are not considering playing off one employer against another. But there are sometimes ways in which you can delay or speed up matters to give yourself possible choices. When an employer makes an offer they frequently seem to think you should drop everything to give an immediate response, forgetting entirely the weeks that have recently passed while you waited to hear whether you were asked to the next stage, when it would be, etc.

But remember! The employer has declared at this stage that they **want you.** The 'want factor' changes everything. For the first time in this relationship you are in charge also of the pace of proceedings.

You may then need to buy time from the organisation that has made the offer. Let them chase you for an answer – they will.

At the conclusion of the second or third job meeting you may be told to expect their offer in writing. The implication is that there will be no negotiating. This is a bluff. Try to negotiate: 'What will it be?' and be prepared to look disappointed. If they do not want to play, you may have to ask for another meeting after receipt of their letter to 'discuss the terms of their offer'. Do not attempt to negotiate over the telephone.

Finally, remember that negotiation is not haggling over money, it is simply normal business practice when buying or selling anything – in this case, your unique services. Many employers have said that people who negotiate well are treated with greater respect and given more opportunities to advance. And in due course you may be negotiating on behalf of the organisation.

The following story was told to me by a client the day an offer letter arrived. It is a while ago so the numbers are low. He was puzzled by the final figure.

Star story

Gary French – a negotiation story

Gary was aged 36 and married. He was an ex-Detective Sergeant in the CID and since had worked as an inquiry agent and as operations director of a vehicle fraud investigation company. He had not earned much money but, in my view, was worth a great deal more than he thought in the right job.

He had had three interviews with an ex-Brit (now Australian) for the job of manager of a debt recovery company – the UK branch (to be set up) of the successful Australian company, now with 4 offices in Australia. Gary thought the salary offered might be around £16–18K and really wanted £20K plus if possible. I had had little success in convincing him he was worth more. This is my transliteration of his verbatim account.

It was the fourth (negotiation of terms) meeting, held in the pub — as chosen by the prospective employer for the earlier meetings.

Australian	There will be a bonus of 10% of the gross profit margin on top of salary.
Gary	(Starts well) That won't be much in year I/II though.
Australian	No, but should be good in years III and IV. Now, what salary are you looking for?
Gary	(Ducks question by saying surely he must have budgeted a figure in his overall plan for the start up.)
Australian	Well, what about £20K?
Gary	(Long silence...mentally saying to himself, 'Golly, this is starting higher than I thought...')
Australian	(Cutting into Gary's thought process) You don't seem very happy about that?
Gary	No, well...(recovers)...I had thought in view of our discussions and the fact that I could bring etc, etc — (90 seconds of job talk followed).
Australian	Well, how about £25K?
Gary	(Mentally gobsmacked! Feels tight knot in stomach) Well...(long pause, while Gary takes it all in).
Australian	I can see you are still not entirely happy. Assuming all goes well we will increase by £3K after three months — and 12 months later we will provide a 2 litre car. Do we have the basis of an agreement?
Gary	(With growing confidence) Yes, I think that does sound like a good basis. If you would just put it all in writing I will give you my formal reply within 48 hours.
Australian	(After pause) I wouldn't have settled for £20K either.

The next day the offer letter arrived containing confirmation with one difference

- bonus of 10% of gross margin
- increase by £3K after 3 months
- 2 litre car 12 months later
- starting salary **not £25K but £27K!**

Gary was quite sure the Australian had made a mistake. Should he point it out he wondered? I argued that it might have been deliberate, to make sure of him. Gary wrote accepting the terms 'as laid out in your letter of...'. We never established the truth for sure. I suggested he might say 'en passant' after checking his first pay cheque. 'Thanks for the extra £2K, it made all the difference.' He did so, but the Australian only grunted. All the terms of the offer were faithfully delivered.

Gary's success was of course mainly accidental. The shock of hearing higher figures than expected thankfully registered as puzzlement (read as disappointment) rather than delight. The Australian, who clearly wanted Gary in the role was probably worried about his try-on figure of £20K even before he started. Gary's two pauses between them sent the salary up by 40% – **such is the power of silence.**

Summary

- Only discuss salary after **fully** negotiating the job and when you are **wanted** for the role.

- Work out your minimum requirements and remember the power of silence.

- Remember that negotiation is a 'game' with rules that are sometimes broken.

- Negotiation is complete when **you** confirm your acceptance in writing.

CHAPTER EIGHT

In the New Position

This chapter looks forward to after the career move. There are immediate matters concerning departure and arrival to deal with, and when the story of how you have changed your job comes to an end a new story begins. A new situation, a new boss and new colleagues suddenly surround you.

This chapter also contains practical advice on how to make the right impact in the new position, plus general advice on management and communication as well as career management.

It also covers final thank you letters.

Leaving and joining

After accepting your new position you have a number of important things to do. If you are in work you must decide when and how to give in your notice. There are others to inform and people to thank. There may be practical large-scale events to manage such as a house to sell and another to buy, but even such a major matter must not be allowed to interfere with certain key requirements.

Do not be tempted to be other than completely courteous and correct in the manner of your leaving your old job. **You do not know how the future will pan out** and in what circumstances you might meet your most loathed colleague again. Perhaps at some point in the future as your boss or most important customer?

More thank you letters

As a result of your job search activities you should now have an expanded personal network. Now is the time to make contact with **all the people you met**, advise them of your success and thank them for their contribution to it. In many cases there is no apparent connection, but anyone's willingness to give you half an hour of their time is in fact a supportive and useful act. In any event people are usually pleased to hear of happy outcomes for others. Also, don't forget to offer your own services for advice and information. A simple sentence will achieve this: 'If you ever need any advice or information that you think I could provide, please don't hesitate to get in touch.' You may be surprised by how many people take up this offer in due course.

Few people seem to think it necessary to advise headhunters or other recruitment agencies of their career moves. This is potentially to miss out badly. If you heard no positive news on this job search occasion, it doesn't mean you won't in the future. Some agencies try to keep their records as up to date as possible and if you advise them of a satisfactory move they can avoid wasting their and your time with any immediate assignments. There are two other advantages for you. They are more likely to remember you for your courtesy in advising them, should some assignment of interest to you come their way, and more likely to agree to see you if and when you want to make another move.

> **Agencies like successful people, in their terms people who get jobs, so let them know about your success.**

The next thing you have to do is turn up at your new place of work and find out what the real job involves. Most employers will have been reasonably honest in their description of the role you are about to fulfil but latterly, given the nature of the job market, they will have been selling it to you without the warts. Now is the time when stones will need to be lifted and strange creatures may scurry out. It is during these early days/weeks/months that you will hear unwelcome news: 'Oh, didn't they tell you about. . . Of course the recent sales figures have been disappointing. . . Surely you knew. . . No, the system has never worked', etc. You will probably be familiar with all this if you can remember how you started your last job.

Starting your new job

Your first and fundamental task is to establish the nature of the environment in which you find yourself. Who does what with whom and to whom and to what purpose? Who has what power and what influence? How are things connected? What do your colleagues, bosses and the people who report to you expect of you, and how will your performance be judged? If you don't know all of this, there is a simple remedy at hand. **You can ask.** Never again will so much indulgence be granted you, so use the opportunity in the early days. You will also find out how much other people do and do not know.

'Start as you mean to go on' is classic advice to people moving into positions of authority, where it is felt you need to assert that authority early or risk never achieving it. Nevertheless it is advice that can apply in any new job, especially when you consider that between a quarter and a third of your life over the next few years is going to be spent working in this new environment. You might as well set out to create the sort of world of work that will suit you. In management-speak this means achieving agreed short- and long-term organisational goals, appropriate self-development, job satisfaction, etc.

Getting on with your boss

Sometimes called 'managing upwards' this is not just a question of maintaining friendly relations with him/her. Nor is it anything to do with manipulating your boss. Rather it is the whole business of discovering what is expected of you, demonstrating what else or what more you can do, and working out together with your boss how your department/section relates to and can work best with the rest of the organisation. In most organisations the hierarchical system obtains in practice if not in theory. Even so-called 'matrix management' systems usually consist of intertwining hierarchies, which work in traditional ways but which change to meet different situations. Generally speaking, your boss will have a boss and, like you, has responsibilities up and down the hierarchy.

You must identify his or her management style quickly and work out what motivates him or her. If it is different from yours you may need to adapt your own style or devote some time and attention to demonstrating how well it complements that of your boss. Whatever differences in style or motivation may exist there are some rules to obey. Do:

- Be punctual.

- Be reachable at all times.

- Be truthful – 'I don't know. I'll find out.'

- Play to your strengths.

◆ Listen. Be aware of how others hear you.

◆ Stick to deadlines. Advise people early if plans are forced off course.

◆ Give **really** bad news as early as possible.

◆ Protect your own staff. You would like your boss to protect you on occasion.

There are books on this topic but these rules and guidelines will see you through.

Managing your staff

Your first action, after any opening meeting with your boss, must be to meet and greet your staff. Unless exceptional circumstances prevail they will not know very much about you. It will help them and you considerably if you can convey, preferably as soon as possible and en masse, something of your style. They need to know how you like to work, what you expect from them, your own short-term plans and a glimpse of your vision if you have one. Then you will need to talk, which means mainly **listen,** to each person individually over the course of the next few hours/days/weeks. Some good ongoing rules include:

◆ Speaking to as many members of staff as possible each day.

◆ Being available between meetings.

◆ Being visible.

◆ Giving praise/thanks in due measure when merited, even for small matters.

◆ Giving individual feedback (positive and negative) regularly and privately.

◆ Demonstrating your commitment to your team and to its objectives.

◆ When under fire assuming initially your team is in the right.

◆ Remembering your staff also have private lives.

◆ Reading some good books on management.

Remember that people are not mind-readers and that it is important to let them know your views, when they are clear. Equally take the time to listen to views from your staff however wrong or daft they may seem initially.

Communicating

Communication lies at the heart of successful work of all kinds. But it takes different forms. If you want to rise to the top of a hierarchical organisation you need to communicate a lot of information upwards about your achievements and your dedication and value to the organisation. If you want to get the best out of your team you will be advising, praising, encouraging and listening to them. Within the operations function of an organisation good communication requires systems that are understood, flexible and which allow all users to see the effect of their input.

General rules of communication, if only we could all manage to obey them all the time, should include:

- Listening to the words, the tone and the intent of the other person.
- Asking questions which enhance understanding.
- Matching style to content, eg 'grave' news.
- Stating your views/perceptions/opinions/wishes/objectives clearly.
- When speaking, listening to yourself and being aware of how others hear you.
- Summarising to check that you/others have understood the same things.
- Considering what might have been said.
- Listening carefully and asking when you do not understand.

Everything works better when people take the trouble to communicate properly.

Making an internal career move

Although your first priority is getting to grips with your new role, if you do start as you mean to go on this will entail:

(a) doing a first class job and

(b) making sure that you get proper credit for so doing.

These are the first two rules of creating the possibility of an internal career move.

Strictly speaking this should be classified as another way to make a career move. It combines networking, self-promotion (though not with a CV), and making unsolicited approaches. Many people think that internal appointments just happen, or not, according to how an organisation happens to develop or change. But **people** change and develop organisations, and as you are one of those people you can have your share of influence.

The value of internal networking

In large organisations and in most public sector areas positions are advertised internally, often before being generally advertised. The rules for applying are the same as for any other advertised job, with the important exceptions that those advertising the position have additional means of finding out about you, and you have additional means of finding out what is involved in the position – i.e. networking.

What follows relates to smaller organisations that do not have a practice of advertising internally or to large organisations who have not yet advertised a position that **you** have identified as suitable for your next move.

Moving jobs within an organisation doesn't happen on the basis of Buggins' turn or luck. If there is a luck element it is mostly created by someone's intelligent application of hard work. Sadly virtue and merit alone are not enough to ensure recognition of your talents. If you want to exercise control over your future career you have to make it happen. Having identified a potential role for yourself you will need to address a number of issues.

Planning your succession

You may not be able to move easily from where you are unless you can leave an acceptable and secure replacement of your function behind you. This may mean reorganising your own area of responsibility as well as considering the needs and wants of your boss and of those who report to you. It will be even easier if you can leave behind a system that will work better or cheaper, or smarter in modern jargon, than the one obtaining when you started your job there. If someone reporting to you could take over your role, or a version of it, remembering that jobs do not have to be 'Charlie shaped', this often provides a neat and happy solution.

The new position

If we assume that this has not yet been generally identified, you are going to have to become known to the peers, contacts and senior people surrounding the area in which the job-to-be sits. You need to work out how it will affect them and try to ensure that this is positive, especially to those concerned who have the most power and influence.

In summary

- ◆ Do a first class job in your current role.

- ◆ Record your achievements in the system.

- ◆ Plan your succession.

- ◆ Try to make it even more cost effective.

- ◆ Let it involve a promotion for someone.

- ◆ Identify your new role and possible timing of an opportunity.

◆ Get yourself known by networking in and around the area of your role-to-be.

◆ Work out what you would bring to the hoped-for new role.

◆ Talk to your boss and talk to your boss's boss about 'possible' moves and help them towards the one you want.

You may of course know all those involved already, as did the creator of the career move in the example below.

Star story

A strategy for a new structure

Peter could see that change was inevitable. As European sales and marketing manager for the largest division in a major international manufacturing company he felt he had been a long time (four years) in a difficult job that was not getting easier. The division was continuing to expand and Peter now had 12 territory managers reporting up through five regional marketing managers. He felt over-burdened with information and day-to-day decisions, not his strong point anyway, and wanted to have a more strategic role and more interaction with his technical counterpart in R&D and with the head of production.

He worked out a way of reorganising the division into two regions so that no one had a significant change of job but his two key regional marketing managers each got increased responsibility and a closer relationship with the plant manager of a single dedicated production unit. The UK regional marketing manager would be recognised as responsible for approximately half the turnover and his continental counterpart suddenly would have his three, erstwhile, colleagues and the whole continental sales operation reporting to him.

Peter tackled his boss, the sales and marketing director, laying stress on the idea that this would speed up decision making between production and sales on all day-to-day matters. His boss liked it, seeing that there would be more time to work on medium- to long-term matters and build closer links with production and R&D.

Peter's boss took soundings at board level, which were favourable, and Peter sold the idea to his reports and to his peers in production and R&D. He got the strategic role he wanted and in effect moved the whole division on.

Summary

♦ After accepting your new position take care how you leave and how you arrive.

♦ **Everyone you have met gets a thank you letter.**

♦ Use the honeymoon period well to ask questions and make mistakes.

♦ Start as you would continue – set out clearly your needs and wants.

♦ Understand the importance of communicating and listening.

♦ Document your progress.

Preparing Your Own CV – a step by step approach

1 The Profile – a pen portrait of yourself

Make a list of your particular **experience** and **expertise** eg process manufacturing industry, PR, warehouse distribution, IT systems design. List also:

- **Skills** – for example, presentation skills, report writing, bookkeeping.

- **Abilities,** sometimes called **transferable skills** – for example, able to analyse complex problems, lead teams by inspiring them, born salesperson.

- **Characteristics/attitudes** – for example, persistence, sunny disposition, achievement-oriented.

You should now have a total list of anything from 15 to 30+ items. All these added together represent a pool of **strengths** from which you can select to market yourself.

Get a friend and/or your spouse or partner, someone whose opinion you respect, or indeed ask several friends, to write down their comments about:

- your strengths

- areas needing a little attention

- what they think would make you happy in your career.

Do not qualify the above statements, nor give them any help at all. And it is no good letting them tell you; they must go away, think and write down their thoughts. When you get each response, **believe it** for the true perception it is. And add the strengths to your own list.

Now write up 6–10 achievements. Take about half a page for each and concentrate on bringing out the actions you took. Whether or not you are achievement-oriented by nature, and some of us are not, you **will have achieved things.** You will have done some things well enough to be able to say, at least to yourself, 'Yes, I did that well'. It doesn't matter whether you found it easy or difficult. We often dismiss what we find easy or what is just part of our job as of little importance but **things you do well** are of interest to others.

Within your achievements you will have been using your particular skills, abilities and experience, **proof** of the reality of your strengths above. As a result of writing them down you may also discover a few strengths, which you missed first time.

Cut your list of strengths down ruthlessly to what you really enjoy doing/what is a key part of your make-up and write an impersonal profile of yourself. Try to find some relevant but unusual element to include, for example:

PROFILE
Raging extrovert with an aptitude for gently sarcastic off-the-cuff remarks, a quick mind, and an excellent memory for faces and names. A good tap dancer and reasonable trombonist. Background in seaside entertainment, at Butlins and Pontins, club hosting and market trading.

Not exactly company secretary material, but a definite prospect for a game show host.

or

PROFILE

A senior executive, with broad administrative experience and a detailed understanding of company law. A practical negotiator both on the shop floor and in the board room, able to maintain concentration over long periods. Background includes 5 years secondment to various government regulatory bodies. Qualified chartered accountant.

Unlikely to host Blind Date, but...

Such a profile, which could be up to twice as long or followed by 5 or 6 bullet points of other key strengths, is designed to be a brief, focused pen-portrait of you in the workplace and what you have to offer. Most of us have about 6–8 key **abilities, or transferable skills.** When you add to these your experience and the **skills** you have learned you should have more than enough raw material. Write too much deliberately and cut it down later.

As far as it goes it must be accurate (check with a good friend). It must serve your objective, the career move you wish to make – which means that it may not be an obviously recognisable portrait of you-as-you-have-been. Your new CV should present you-as-you-are-and-can-become. Its purpose is to propel you forwards not hold you back.

2 Achievements

In turn, the profile should be supported by factual data, expressed in the form of achievements. These should be brief accounts of three to five achievements which support/illustrate the strengths claimed in the **PROFILE.** Achievement story length should be about 30–40 words, and it is a good idea to give each achievement story a title. You can have fun with the titles and inform people at the same time.

Titles for such a section could be:

RECENT/SELECTED/SUPPORTING ACHIEVEMENTS – pick and/or mix – or

CAREER HIGHLIGHTS, especially when including items which are not technically achievements, eg:

Diplomacy at the highest level

Chosen to represent our (British) company at international conference in Las Vegas celebrating 200 years of one-armed bandit manufacturing. Delivered keynote speech to the 2000+ delegates.

Making a separate section for achievements draws attention to them. If you do not wish to do this, use the more traditional approach and record them in shorter form in the main section under **CAREER DETAILS, CAREER HISTORY, WORK EXPERIENCE,** or **CAREER PROGRESSION** – use whichever title you prefer. Focus under each job title on achievements rather than on duties or responsibilities and quantify them when possible.

3 Career details – the main section

This layout format works well when incorporating achievements under career details.

PROFILE

Senior executive with worldwide experience of business-to-business negotiations at the highest level. A fluent communicator in four languages, with a record of setting and meeting ambitious targets, currently looking for new role in an international context requiring diplomatic and analytical strengths. Other key strengths include:

- Strong leadership and team building abilities.
- First class administrative and budgetary skills.

- An intuitive approach to identifying problems and opportunities.
- Calm and patient under pressure.

CAREER PROGRESSION

1999–date   EXWHYZED COMPANY LTD (worldwide plastic components)
t/o. £350m

  03–0X **Sales & marketing director** 45 staff

     Reorganised distribution worldwide following European model
     Led team in acquisition of ELEMEN Paper and Plastics Inc. for
     £100m
     Chairman of the International Paper Federation (elected 1999)

  99–03 **Marketing director – Europe** t/o. £68m, 14 staff, 3 direct reports
     Responsible for marketing and sales in UK and all of continental
     Europe

     Increased sales by average of 10% p.a. over 4 years and profit
     contribution by 3% p.a. Now market leader
     Developed distribution channels in new territories and opened
     marketing offices in France and Germany

1993–1999   AHBEYCEY PLASTIQUE S.A. Paris t/o. FF 80m (£10m)
  96–99 **Sales manager** – France, Spain and Italy

     Set up first market research studies to identify new market sectors
     Increased sales by 25% over 3 years

  93–96 **Commercial manager** (factory based)

     Set up new computerised order planning system, saving 18 man
     hours per wk.
     Reduced lead times by 50% to 3 weeks for all standard lines (80%
     of output)

1987–1993 UK MACHINE TOOLS LTD

    91–93 **European representative**
    89–91 **Sales administrator**
    87–88 **Technical graduate trainee**

You can highlight whatever you want simply by varying use of capital letters and bold. It is sometimes argued that caps are not so legible as lower case. I would argue that names of companies and organisations are often written in capital letters and not too difficult to read. CV section headings are here differentiated by bold caps and job titles by bold sentence case for quick and easy identification anywhere on the page.

By convention this main section of the CV is written in reverse order, with more detail given about the most recent positions, i.e. the last 7–12 years. In the case of a long career and/or many jobs it may be sensible to collapse early jobs, especially when irrelevant to your current objective, into a sentence such as:

  Early career in stockbroking/retail management/the transport
  industry. . .(include the names of any well-regarded employers). . .with **Hoare
  Govett/Marks and Spencer/Danzas International.**

Clarity and layout

The use of clearly understandable job titles will save a lot of words describing duties. If your title describes your job inadequately, change it to one which does it better. This is not dishonest so long as you do not steal an existing title from a colleague; it is a way of more accurately informing your reader.

It is a usually a good idea to indicate the size and scope of the job. Turnover, budget size, numbers of staff managed, etc, all can be expressed in figures next to company/division or job title, as appropriate.

Spend time and thought on layout. Leave plenty of space around the headings. Be careful with line breaks. It is really irritating to a reader to have to turn back a page to find a missing sub-heading. Good layout helps the reader, which helps you.

If in the career details section you use years (1990–1996) rather than years and months (September 1990 – February 1996) it might disguise a six month employment gap **you** feel uncomfortable about. Much more importantly you take up less space, give your reader less to process and present a less cluttered page. In the unlikely event that you are asked to supply months at an interview, simply give them. Your interviewer should and will be much more interested in how you meet their needs today than in what happened between your jobs in 1990 or 1996.

4 Additional supporting data

The main career section will be followed by further background information to complete a rounded picture of you as a whole person. Headings used could include:

EDUCATION/QUALIFICATIONS/TRAINING – pick and/or mix. Highest levels first, GCSE/'O' Levels unspecified or omitted unless highest level.

LANGUAGES – indicate fluency level.

COMPUTER LITERACY – technical/IT people may need a separate page or pages.

PUBLICATIONS – separate sheet if lengthy/vital to your cause.

ADDITIONAL ACTIVITIES – eg school governor/parish councillor.

INTERESTS – not too many, variety helps – include any genuine passion.

PERSONAL DETAILS – marital status, health ('excellent' is best), date of birth. Good reason/reasons of principle needed for leaving out any of these.

5 Objective – optional

Optional, that is, in the sense that you may or may not feature it on your CV. However, if you have no objective you will usually arrive somewhere else!

If you state an objective, it should appear as the first item on your CV, even if it may be the last item to be clarified in your mind. Once you have a short-term career objective everything about job searching becomes easier. It should describe some or all of the following items:

♦ The role, its level or seniority.

♦ The size of organisation.

♦ The area of business/industry/commerce/activity/public/private sector.

♦ Your main contribution or activity.

The main reason for putting a written objective on the CV is to help other people to understand what you want to do and thus be better able to help you in your job search. It is very useful when networking, especially in early stages when you may wish to establish more precision about career direction and when your objective may be vague. The degree of precision an objective has may vary considerably. For example:

OBJECTIVE
A position as HR Director in a large IT company where my experience in USA and Canada and my compensation/benefits expertise will be fully exploited (**very precise**).

or

OBJECTIVE

A senior executive role, in a medium- to large-sized organisation, possibly with international connections, where my analytical and high level negotiating skills will be used to identify and develop profitable business to business activity (**somewhat vague**).

Modifications

If you compile your CV as outlined above you should not need to modify it for individual applications.

Exceptions to this might be the substitution of a particular achievement story by another more apposite one or the modification of your objective if your CV carries one. You may, for example, have been very focused on a particular sector, specified in your CV, only to discover an additional sector where you have found a job you could do equally well.

There is also a case to be made for changing the wording of your objective if it fits too exactly the employer's own description. Quite simply you may not be believed. It may be better to de-focus it slightly or even leave it off. Whenever you apply for a particular job you are saying by implication that the job meets your objectives. In any case your CV should never travel alone. If not accompanied by you it should always have a covering letter, and this covering letter is the main vehicle for focusing on a particular position.

> **The less we write about ourselves, the more remarkable and powerful it often seems to be.**

Try to keep your CV to a maximum of three pages – two is better. When deciding what to put in/leave out try to think back to the purposes of the CV.

Does it promote you? Is it useful to the reader? 'If in doubt, leave it out' is a good rule for CVs. There is much advantage in leaving the reader wanting more.

> **Secret tip**
>
> If, however, you are really desperate to write four pages there is a neat way of achieving it with a one-page document. You take your sheets of A4 and photocopy pages 2 and 3 onto one side of a piece of good quality paper, A3 size, and pages 4 and 1 (think about it) onto the other side. Then fold in half. One sheet of paper and lots of space.

Psychometrics

Career problems are life problems

'Once upon a time life was much simpler...' It is always tempting to look back at a golden age or to select real examples from the past where life and work was indeed simple but which may be difficult to repeat today. For example, a country doctor's son goes off to medical school to qualify, comes back to join and then take over father's practice, meanwhile marrying the vicar's daughter, his childhood sweetheart, who after teaching in the village school settles down to produce a family...

The point is not that life was necessarily simpler but that there were more and clearer patterns, if fewer choices. In theory at least today's young managers and professionals have a vastly enhanced potential for choice and freedom – not for these the country doctor's furrow.

So what happens?

Today young men and women around the 30–35 year age group, earning anything between £30k and £300k p.a. in industry, commerce, the professions and in the City would seem to have arrived, to have the world at their feet. I refer here to the bright ones, those who are good at something that is valued by their employers. If it appears to outsiders or even to themselves that some are overpaid for what they do so be it, they carry the label of success.

The problem arises when success no longer satisfies. Our working life successful or otherwise is only one aspect of our life and inevitably connected to the rest of who we are and what we do.

Most of us:

♦ Have interests outside our work which may or may not be related to our work. An IT 'rocket scientist' may surf the net out of hours compulsively, or simply when needing a piece of information connected with, say, an interest in mediaeval tapestries.

♦ Have or seek relationships of a loving and/or sexual nature. Often the working environment is a fruitful source of such relationships.

♦ Come to a point where we want to put down some roots, take on some permanent/ongoing responsibilities in connection with a partner and/or children.

When success is an enabling factor in fulfilling interests and relationship requirements there is rarely a problem. We pick up our partner in the BMW and carry him/her off to our Docklands loft to raise children, restore the country cottage and move on steadily to become chief executive. If, however, despite clearing the mortgage or accumulating six or seven figures worth of cash and/or shares by the age of 32, we are working 12 hours a day, and in an iffy on/off relationship, the situation may look and feel very different.

The problem is particularly acute for women for whom there are so few role models. Their parents simply did not have today's opportunities. Those fifteen to twenty years older, Thatcher's mid-to-late eighties brood, were the groundbreakers, but there was no pattern to their groundbreaking.

The women who crashed into and through the glass ceiling have left fragile areas and gaping holes. It is not the problem it was to get through but there is no blueprint for how to handle it all up in the stratosphere. And does everyone want the stratosphere anyway?

Many young women and men seem to have it all, but what they sometimes do not have is their own sense of balance and control. Somehow, whilst the career blossomed and the money rolled in, it did not seem to matter, or it could be sorted out later. When redundancy appears, or the partner disappears, or simply when work begins to lose the power to stimulate, the questions pile in. Where am I going? How do I get off this treadmill? How much time have I got? What do I really want? How do I restore some balance and what do I want to balance with what? When families are involved or potential families are being planned or thought about, the equations are even more complex. So what to do?

In such a situation, which could be described as an early or mid-career life crisis, there may be many factors involved or a single one. Help is needed for people to stand back from the noise and confusion of their immediate situation and focus on their core needs and wants. If there is no convenient role model, you may have to be your own, and whatever you do you have to be true to yourself and to whatever drives you.

It is difficult for some people to get through such a crisis on their own. Others, with just a little input from one or two friends/colleagues sail through it. How is this so? The reasons have to lie in the differences between people. It is but a step from here to the controversial matter of the value and dangers of 'typology'.

The Myers-Briggs Type Indicator® (MBTI®) instrument

Some people object violently to the idea of being 'typed'. If it involves being given a label that acts as a straightjacket I should also object. However we constantly categorise people without recourse to any theory to back it up:

> 'Brian will always sit on the fence rather than make a decision. He can always find a reason for not acting now. And if you scotch his reason he will come up with three others.'

Several people who all know Brian very well may have no difficulty in agreeing with this statement. The only error in this kind of thinking lies in the use of words like **always, never, constantly, only**, etc. Whatever our 'type' we can choose to act against its apparent dictates.

The MBTI® instrument was created and developed in the 1950s by Isabel Myers and her mother Katherine Briggs based on the psychological type theory of Carl Jung. It looks at certain key preferences that we have concerning how we like to perceive the world around us, and how we make judgements. This is also the process by which we interpret the world and make sense of it. These preferences also colour our judgement strongly. When Mandy Rice-Davies said of John Profumo's denial of an affair with Christine Keeler, 'He would, wouldn't he?' she was referring to his situation not his type but the phrase could refer to many of us when our actions reflect our type.

The theory

Jung's theory proposed eight types based on three bi-polar axes or opposite pairs of preferences: extraversion and introversion (E/I), sensing and iNtuition (S/N), and thinking and feeling (T/F). Katherine Briggs added a fourth, a preference for either the judging or the perceiving process (J/P). This then allowed for sixteen types, usually arranged as follows.

	SENSING TYPES			**INTUITIVE TYPES**		
	Thinking	**Feeling**		**Feeling**	**Thinking**	
With						
	IS<u>T</u>J	IS<u>F</u>J		IN<u>F</u>J	IN<u>T</u>J	**Judging**
			I N T R O V E R T S			
	IS<u>T</u>P	IS<u>F</u>P		IN<u>F</u>P	IN<u>T</u>P	**Perceiving**
	ES<u>T</u>P	ES<u>F</u>P		EN<u>F</u>P	EN<u>T</u>P	**Perceiving**
			E X T R A V E R T S			
	ES<u>T</u>J	ES<u>F</u>J		EN<u>F</u>J	EN<u>T</u>J	**Judging**

Underlined letters represent the dominant preference for each type.

There is much to explore in the MBTI® assessment tool. A good place to start is to read the book by Isabel Briggs Myers and Peter B Myers (her son), *Gifts Differing* (Davies-Black Publishing) 1995, 3rd edition.

Type and career counselling

There is only space here to give a flavour of Myers-Briggs typology. Here are a couple of examples:

ISTJ indicates an Introverted Sensing type with Thinking preferring Judging. This is the kind of person who is interested in detail, who does things by the book and who likes to make plans and decisions. If I wanted my car serviced or a long and complicated, routine operation performed on my brain I would like it done by an ISTJ, please.

The opposite type is ENFP, an Extraverted iNtuitive type with Feeling preferring Perceiving. Such a person is often good at creating new ways of approaching situations, is interested in possibilities, likes ambiguity and is flexible and adaptable, an ideal type to breathe some life into new product development. Most ISTJs would make rather heavy weather of such an assignment though they would go about it systematically and conscientiously.

There are so-called 'planners' and 'adapters', 'leaders' and 'nurturers'. People have natural preferences and abilities and usually are happiest and most productive when choosing and using them.

Fifteen years of one-to-one work with clients with known MBTI® profiles have convinced me that people benefit from understanding their preferences in perceiving and making judgements in ways that are useful to them in their everyday dealings with others and therefore in the workplace. An understanding of type is also useful in helping people to realise how colleagues and bosses prefer to take in information. Is it 'broad brush' or detail? How do they like to make decisions? Are they focused more on facts or on possibilities?

Unsurprisingly the mix of 'types' seeking career counselling appears to be different from the population as a whole. Having worked with some very different kinds of organisation I can also attest to some very strong trends of an apparently perplexing nature.

♦ In the early and mid-nineties about 20% of my clients at Chusid Lander Inc. came out as introverted thinking types (ISTJ). EN-Ps, adaptable intuitive types, were about 3%.

♦ During the last four years of the nineties, working with Jo Ouston & Co I would estimate that about 50% of my clients (on average 10 years younger) were selecting the two EN-P categories or were feeling types. ISTJs numbered perhaps 5%.

As an ENFP type I believe I know exactly how this came about (I would, wouldn't I). The majority of Chusid Lander clients were paying for a precise methodology to get an even better job than their last or current one. My recent EN-P clients at Jo Ouston & Co have a lot of career choice and are looking for a creative exploration of their options and possibilities and to find focus – different people on different missions.

This anecdotal evidence is not designed to convince anyone of anything other than that samples do tend to self-select and that certain attitudes seem to be ingrained in certain Myers-Briggs types.

People seek career counselling for many different reasons, according to the sort of people they are:

♦ Some believe that whenever possible in life one should consult an 'expert' on the basis that a professional approach will lead to better results. (*ISTJs, INTJs, ESTJs, ENTJs.*)

♦ Some lack confidence or self-belief and feel the need of support and encouragement from a mentor. (*No type and every type. Though it is my experience that many of the most successful high achievers will often admit privately to a deep and deeply buried lack of confidence in themselves. If so it usually fuels the next success.*)

◆ Some do not know what they want to do, except it should not be what they have been doing so far. (*Any P, especially INFP, also sometimes INFJs.*)

◆ Some feel themselves to be at a crossroads and want advice about which of two, three or sometimes four ways they should go. (*Any type who is ambitious or career minded.*)

◆ Some are not enjoying what they are doing, who believe there are various options open to them, but can't seem to see a career plan for themselves. Many have landed all their jobs to date more or less by accident. (*Lots of talented ENFPs and ENTPs in this group. They often have a lot of genuine career choice, hence the difficulty.*)

◆ Some want advice and instruction on some or all aspects of how to get the job they have set their heart or mind on. (*These people don't need career advice but they do need **job search guidance**, as do most of the rest, because it is not taught at school or university.*)

Some effects of type differences

The tables on the following pages are modified and reproduced by special permission of the Publisher, CPP Inc, Palo Alto, CA 94303 from *Gifts Differing*, by Isabel Briggs Myers with Peter B. Myers. Copyright 1995 by Davies-Black Publishing, a division of CPP Inc. All rights reserved. Further reproduction is prohibited without the publisher's written consent. You may have some fun by finding on each page the column of statements with which you more closely identify. This is not a test, just an exercise. If you want to find out what your own type is you should get in touch with a licensed MBTI® administrator.

Effects of extraversion–introversion at work

Extraverts:	*Introverts:*
Like variety and action.	Like quiet for concentration.
Tend to work fast, dislike complicated procedures.	Tend to be careful with details, dislike sweeping statements.
Are often good at greeting people.	Have trouble remembering names and faces.
Are often impatient with long slow jobs.	Tend not to mind working on one project for a long time uninterruptedly.
Are interested in the results of their job, in getting it done, and in how other people do it.	Are interested in the idea behind their job.
Often do not mind the interruption of answering the telephone.	Dislike telephone intrusions and interruptions.
Often act quickly, sometimes without thinking.	Like to think a lot before they act, sometimes without acting.
Like to have people around.	Work contentedly alone.
Usually communicate freely.	Have some problems communicating.

Are you more E   or   **I?**

Effects of sensing–intuition at work

Sensing types:

Dislike new problems unless there are standard ways to solve them.

Like an established way of doing things.

Enjoy using skills already learned more than learning new ones.

Work more steadily, with a realistic idea of how long it will take.

Usually reach a conclusion step by step.

Are patient with routine details.

Are impatient when the details get complicated.

Are not often inspired, and rarely trust the inspiration when they are inspired.

Seldom make errors of fact.

Tend to be good at precise work.

Intuitive types:

Like solving new problems.

Dislike doing the same thing repeatedly.

Enjoy learning a new skill more than using it.

Work in bursts of energy, powered by enthusiasm, with slack periods in between.

Reach a conclusion quickly.

Are impatient with routine details.

Are patient with complicated situations.

Follow their inspirations, good or bad.

Frequently make errors of fact.

Dislike taking time for precision.

Are you more S or **N?**

Effects of thinking–feeling at work

Thinking types:

Do not show emotion readily and are often uncomfortable dealing with people's feelings.

May hurt people's feelings without knowing it.

Like analysis and putting things into logical order. Can get along without harmony.

Tend to decide impersonally sometimes paying insufficient attention to people's wishes.

Need to be treated fairly.

Are able to reprimand people or fire them when necessary.

Are more analytically oriented – respond more easily to people's thoughts.

Tend to be firm-minded.

Feeling types:

Tend to be very aware of other people and their feelings.

Enjoy pleasing people, even in unimportant things.

Like harmony. Efficiency may be badly disrupted by office feuds.

Often let decisions be influenced by their own or other people's personal likes and dislikes.

Need occasional praise.

Dislike telling people unpleasant things.

Are more people oriented – respond more easily to people's values.

Tend to be sympathetic.

Are you more T or **F?**

Effects of judgment–perception at work

Judging types:	*Perceptive types:*
Work best when they can plan their work and follow the plan.	Adapt well to changing situations.
Like to get things settled and finished.	Do not mind leaving things open for alterations.
May decide things too quickly.	May have trouble making decisions.
May dislike to interrupt the project they are on for a more urgent one.	May start too many projects and have difficulty in finishing them.
May not notice new things that need to be done.	May postpone unpleasant jobs.
Want only the essentials needed to begin their work.	Want to know all about a new job.
Tend to be satisfied once they reach a judgment on a thing, situation or person.	Tend to be curious and welcome a new light on a thing, situation, or person.

Are you more J or **P?**

Note: Remember, this exercise has no psychological validity. If you want to discover your true Myers-Briggs type you should apply to a professional, licensed MBTI® administrator.

Career drivers

Just as people have particular preferences, which relate to the kinds of choices they may make with respect to their career, so they usually have some particular inner drivers, motivating goals that drive them to achieve either straightforward externally recognisable objectives such as material wealth or a level at which to perform, eg expertise, or even states of being such as security. I have picked here the career drivers related to the work of Professor Edgar Schein of MIT on career anchors, though there are other models of things which may guide us in our careers.

Professor Schein's model is actually somewhat differently expressed. He writes about 'career anchors', of which he identifies eight, including six which closely match six of the career drivers. Rather than being something that drives you a career anchor is described as 'that one element in a person's self-concept that he or she will not give up, even in the face of difficult choices'. (*Career Anchors – Discovering your real values*, by Edgar H. Schein, 1990.) Professor Schein's work is based on an in depth study of 44 alumni from the Master's programme at the Sloan School of Management from 1961 through to 1973.

For those of us who are not **achievement** driven as most of modern business would have us be, and I count myself firmly in that camp, it may come as a surprise that we are driven at all. In this model nine distinct drivers are identified, which are combinations of needs and wants. They identify what people are looking for and what their key concern is in connection with their work.

They are as follows:

Driver	*What is sought*	*Key concern*
Material wealth	Possessions and a high standard of living	Wealth
Power and influence	Control of people and resources	Dominance

Meaning	Doing things believed to be intrinsically valuable	Contribution
Expertise	A high level of specialised accomplishment	Mastery
Creativity	Innovating and being identified with innovations	Originality
Affiliation	Nourishing relationships at work	Closeness
Autonomy	Being independent and able to decide for oneself	Own choice
Security	A solid and predictable future	Assurance
Status	Recognition and respect from the community	Position and symbols

Career drivers are held to be basic components of our individual identity. If this is so we ignore our drivers at our peril. The test, 'Analyse your career motivation' (pp 156–162), pairs statements supporting every driver with every other driver. Like many other tests it is useless as a recruitment tool, as most people will supply the answers thought to be most likely to get the job. However when people do it for themselves it often provides a new insight or two. The scoring system forces a result, and most people emerge with two or three drivers with only one at the core.

You can complete the test in about 10–15 minutes.

Before you start

You are asked to evaluate the relative importance to you of the following pairs of statements by allocating three points to each pair. You must allocate all three points and no more than three. Thus you have four choices:

First statement   3   2   1   0

Second statement   0   1   2   3

Choose the one most appropriate for you. Ignore the letters given for each statement. These are for scoring later.

A word of warning – you will sooner or later find yourself struggling to decide how to mark two statements, both of which, or neither of which apply to you. Don't worry. Just persist and make one of your four allowed choices even if it seems arbitrary.

There are of course no right or wrong answers. If you have real difficulty in deciding between a particular pair leave it and go back later. Work as quickly as you can through the thirty-six pairs. Ten to fifteen minutes is usually enough time.

Analyse your career motivation

1.   A _____   I will only be satisfied with an unusually high standard of living.

    B _____   I wish to have considerable influence over other people.

2.   C _____   I only feel satisfied if the output from my job has real value in itself.

    D _____   I want to be an expert in the things I do.

3.   E _____   I want to use my creative abilities in my work.

    F _____   It is specially important to me that I work with people who I like.

4.   G _____   I would obtain particular satisfaction by being able to freely choose what I do.

    H _____   I want to make sure I will be financially secure.

5.   A _____   Not to put too fine a point on it, I want to be wealthy.

    I _____   I enjoy feeling that people look up to me.

6.   B _____   I want a substantial leadership role.

    C _____   I do that which is meaningful to me, even though it may not gain tangible rewards.

7. D _____ I want to feel that I have gained a hard-won expertise.

   E _____ I want to create things which people associate with me alone.

8. F _____ I seek deep social relationships with other people in my work.

   G _____ I would get satisfaction from deciding how I spend my time.

9. A _____ I will not be content until I have ample material possessions.

   D _____ I want to demonstrate to my own satisfaction that I really know my discipline.

10. C _____ My work is part of my search for meaning in life.

   E _____ I want the things that I produce to bear my name.

11. A _____ I seek to be able to afford anything I want.

   H _____ A job with long-term security really appeals to me.

12. B _____ I seek a role which gives me substantial influence over others.

   D _____ I would enjoy being a specialist in my field.

13. C _____ It is important to me that my work makes a positive contribution to the wider community.

   F _____ Close relationships with other people at work are important to me.

14. E _____ I want my personal creativity to be extensively used.

   G _____ I would prefer to be my own master.

15. F _____ Closer relationships with other people at work would give me special satisfaction.

   H _____ I want to look ahead in my life and feel confident I will always be OK.

16. A _____ I want to be able to spend money easily.

   E _____ I want to be genuinely innovative in my work.

17. B _____ Frankly, I want to tell other people what to do.

   F _____ For me being close to others is the really important thing.

18. C _____ I look on my career as part of a search for greater meaning in life.

    G _____ I have found I want to have full responsibility for my own decisions.

19. D _____ I would enjoy a reputation as a real specialist.

    H _____ I would feel relaxed if I was in a secure career.

20. A _____ I desire the trappings of wealth.

    F _____ I want to get to know new people through my work.

21. B _____ I like to play roles which give me control over how others perform.

    G _____ It is important for me that I choose for myself the tasks that I undertake.

22. C _____ I would devote myself to work if I believed that the output would be worthwhile in itself.

    H _____ I would take great comfort from knowing how I will stand on retirement day.

23. F _____ Close relationships with people at work would make it difficult for me to make a career move.

    I _____ Being recognised as part of the 'establishment' is important to me.

24. B _____ I would enjoy being in charge of people and resources.

    E _____ I want to create things that no one else has done before.

25. C _____ At the end of the day I do what is important, not what simply promotes my career.

    I _____ I seek public recognition.

26. E _____ I want to do something distinctly different from others.

    H _____ I usually take the soft option.

27. B _____ I want people to look to me for leadership.

    I _____ Social status is an important motivator for me.

28. A _____ High standard of living attracts me.

    G _____ I wish to avoid being tightly controlled by a boss at work.

29. E _____ I want my products to have my own name on them.

    I _____ I seek from others formal recognition of my achievements.

30. B _____ I prefer to be in charge.

    H _____ I feel concerned when I cannot see a long way ahead in my career.

31. D _____ I would enjoy being a person who had valuable specialist knowledge.

    G _____ I would get satisfaction from not having to answer to other people.

32. G _____ I dislike being a cog in a large wheel.

    I _____ It would give me satisfaction to have a high-status job.

33. A _____ I am prepared to do most things for material reward.

    C _____ I seek work as a means of enriching my personal development.

34. H _____ A secure future attracts me every time.

    I _____ I want to have a prestigious position in any organisation in which I work.

35. D _____ Being able to make an expert contribution would give me particular satisfaction.

    F _____ When I have good social relationships nothing else really matters.

36. D _____ I aspire to a high level of specialist competence.

    I _____ I would enjoy the status symbols which come with senior positions.

To analyse your career motivation follow the scoring instructions on page 160.

Score sheet

Take your scores from each pair in the questionnaire and put them in the appropriate column. Add up each column and check that the sum of all the columns is 108. If it is not you have made one or more of the following errors:

◆ not allocated three points to each pair
◆ made a transposition error filling in this sheet
◆ added up incorrectly

	A	B	C	D	E	F	G	H	I
1.	—	—	.	.	.	.	.	.	.
2.	.	.	—	—	.	.	.	.	.
3.	.	.	.	.	—	—	.	.	.
4.	.	.	.	.	.	.	—	—	.
5.	—	.	.	.	.	.	.	.	—
6.	.	—	—	.	.	.	.	.	.
7.	.	.	.	—	—	.	.	.	.
8.	.	.	.	.	.	—	—	.	.
9.	—	.	.	—	.	.	.	.	.
10.	.	.	—	.	—	.	.	.	.
11.	—	.	.	.	.	.	.	—	.
12.	.	—	.	—	.	.	.	.	.
13.	.	.	—	.	.	—	.	.	.
14.	.	.	.	.	—	.	—	.	.
15.	.	.	.	.	.	—	.	—	.
16.	—	.	.	.	—	.	.	.	.

	A	B	C	D	E	F	G	H	I
17.	·	—	·	·	·	—	·	·	·
18.	·	·	—	·	·	·	—	·	·
19.	·	·	·	—	·	·	·	—	·
20.	—	·	·	·	·	—	·	·	·
21.	·	—	·	·	·	·	—	·	·
22.	·	·	—	·	·	·	·	—	·
23.	·	·	·	·	·	—	·	·	—
24.	·	—	·	·	—	·	·	·	·
25.	·	·	—	·	·	·	·	·	—
26.	·	·	·	·	—	·	·	—	·
27.	·	—	·	·	·	·	·	·	—
28.	—	·	·	·	·	·	—	·	·
29.	·	·	·	·	—	·	·	·	—
30.	·	—	·	·	·	·	·	—	·
31.	·	·	·	—	·	·	—	·	·
32.	·	·	·	·	·	·	—	·	—
33.	—	·	—	·	·	·	·	·	·
34.	·	·	·	·	·	·	·	—	—
35.	·	·	·	—	·	—	·	·	·
36.	·	·	·	—	·	·	·	·	—

Total

Now plot your results on the next page.

Career Drivers Profile

	A	B	C	D	E	F	G	H	I
24	+	+	+	+	+	+	+	+	+
23	+	+	+	+	+	+	+	+	+
22	+	+	+	+	+	+	+	+	+
21	+	+	+	+	+	+	+	+	+
20	+	+	+	+	+	+	+	+	+
19	+	+	+	+	+	+	+	+	+
18	+	+	+	+	+	+	+	+	+
17	+	+	+	+	+	+	+	+	+
16	+	+	+	+	+	+	+	+	+
15	+	+	+	+	+	+	+	+	+
14	+	+	+	+	+	+	+	+	+
13	+	+	+	+	+	+	+	+	+
12	+	+	+	+	+	+	+	+	+
11	+	+	+	+	+	+	+	+	+
10	+	+	+	+	+	+	+	+	+
9	+	+	+	+	+	+	+	+	+
8	+	+	+	+	+	+	+	+	+
7	+	+	+	+	+	+	+	+	+
6	+	+	+	+	+	+	+	+	+
5	+	+	+	+	+	+	+	+	+
4	+	+	+	+	+	+	+	+	+
3	+	+	+	+	+	+	+	+	+
2	+	+	+	+	+	+	+	+	+
1	+	+	+	+	+	+	+	+	+
0	+	+	+	+	+	+	+	+	+
	A	B	C	D	E	F	G	H	I

A   Material rewards

B   Power and influence

C   Meaning

D   Expertise

E   Creativity

F   Affiliation

G   Autonomy

H   Security

I   Status

The drivers

(A) Material rewards

Seeking possessions and a high standard of living. Key concern – wealth.

Material rewards are defined as tangible assets and include money, quality of furnishings, quality of car, and other material possessions. People with this driver take decisions about future work primarily to enhance their material well being. They seek roles that provide a high income (and perks). They may take jobs which are unfulfilling but which provide a high income and benefits or other material rewards.

The yuppies of Britain and America are prime examples of people driven by *material rewards*. Devoted to the pursuit of wealth they were fastidious about their dress and possessions and took enormous interest in investments, taxation and other financial areas of their lives.

(B) Power and influence

Seeking to be in control of people and resources. Key concern – dominance.

Power and influence is defined as wanting to be dominant and to have others behave in subordinate roles. It is also connected with wanting to take decisions about policy and how resources are used.

People who have this driver take decisions primarily to increase the extent of their personal control over people and situations. They attempt to move towards the centre of organisations and gain formal as well as informal power. They get great satisfaction from deciding what is to be done and who is going to do it. They are often uncomfortable in subordinate roles where control is tightly organised by their boss.

People with *power and influence* as a key driver seem to gravitate towards managerial or political roles. They are proactive. They use their power and influence. They are self-confident in their behaviour and clear about what should be done.

(C) Search for meaning

Seeking to do things which are believed valuable for their own sake. Key concern – contribution.

Search for meaning is defined as being motivated to do things finer or greater than the individual according to religious, emotional, social or intellectual criteria. People with this driver will take decisions that can only be explained in the context of their personal beliefs and values. This could take the form of helping others rather than helping themselves. Personal fulfilment is their ultimate pay-off. They may make considerable sacrifices in order to follow their inner beliefs.

The *search for meaning* is sometimes connected with other drivers rather than standing alone.

(D) Expertise

Seeking a high level of accomplishment in a specialised field. Key concern – mastery.

Expertise is defined as specialist knowledge, skills, know-how, competence and capacity to perform unusual, difficult or specialised activities.

People with this driver work hard to gain a depth of competence in limited or specialist fields and will strive to maintain their specialist role. They dislike going outside their specialist area. One of their primary sources of satisfaction is being regarded and valued as an expert. The expertise can be in just about anything, it might be a physical skill, technical ability or academic knowledge. Thus a blacksmith, a chemist and a university professor might all have expertise as a primary driver. Professional managers can also be included in this category.

People driven by *expertise* will structure their working lives around a discipline. The context and challenge of the work determines their behaviour. Generally professional or trade qualifications are seen as essential. The specialist likes to keep up to date with journals, conferences, study programmes, etc.

(E) Creativity

Seeking to innovate and be identified with original output. Key concern – originality.

Creativity is defined as creating something new which bears the name of the originator. This may be a work of science, art, literature, an entrepreneurial activity or even a form of entertainment. People with this driver do things which are distinctly different from things that other people do, and want to own the results. The individual's name is closely associated with his or her products. Genuine innovation is highly prized.

People with *creativity* as a key driver will derive excitement from breaking new ground. They are stimulated by puzzles, riddles, challenges and problems. They can take setbacks and failures without destroying their sense of optimism. The feeling of accomplishing something novel or new is what they seek. People with this driver are willing to take decisions to their disadvantage if it allows them to working a creative role. They often prefer a solitary or small team environment.

(F) Affiliation

Seeking nourishing relationships with others at work. Key concern – closeness.

Affiliation is defined as striving to be close to others, enjoying the bonds of friendship and being enriched by human relationships. People with this career driver take steps to develop deep and fulfilling relationships with others. These bonds become extremely important to them. They put their feelings for others before self and preserve continuity in important relationships. They may put up with unfulfilling jobs because of the quality of their relationships with their colleagues. Their commitment is to people and not to tasks, position or organisational goals.

(G) Autonomy

Seeking to be independent and able to make decisions for oneself. Key concern – own choice.

Autonomy is defined as taking personal responsibility for the structure, processes and objectives of daily life. People with this driver act to increase the amount of control they have over their own working lives. They resist attempts to organise them and put them into a 'box'. People like this often fail to cope with bureaucracy and seek to become their own masters. They enjoy feeling 'I did it all', and prefer to work alone or with a small team which they lead.

The desire for independence is very influential in people driven by *autonomy*. They do not like to be directed by others. Procedures, systems and protocols are seen as irritants. Restrictions evoke hostility or fury. Sometimes these people can function happily in organisations if they can negotiate a good deal of psychological space for themselves. This type of person will sacrifice organisational position for self-direction. Those who are 'self-made' often have *autonomy* as a career driver.

(H) Security

Seeking a solid and predictable future. Key concern – assurance.

Security is defined as wanting to know the future and to avoid being exposed to risks. People with this driver take decisions which help them to feel relaxed about their future. Their primary goal is high predictability rather than high income. They see life as a journey to be undertaken with the best maps and guides available.

This type of person chooses employers after careful consideration of their stability and record of looking after their employees. They may associate security with working for blue chip companies and institutions. They make career decisions and choices with the future in mind. If a promotion opportunity substantially increases doubt about their future they may well reject it.

People driven by *security* accept the world as it is. They evade decisions and conflicts that could make or break. They undergo training to increase their worth to their organisation. Security does not necessarily mean staying with one company. A *security* driven person may change companies several times to broaden their experience to increase their marketability to help ensure that they will always be able to get a job.

(l) Status

Seeking to be recognised, admired and respected by the community at large. Key concerns – position and status symbols.

Status is defined as wanting the esteem of others, and to be highly regarded. Status is demonstrated by symbols, formal recognition and acceptance into privileged groups.

People with *status* as a career driver undertake whatever actions are needed to enhance their prestige. This includes making personal contacts with influential people, taking responsible assignments and self-publicising. They may seek positions of power and authority, but their desire is for the prestige of the position rather than the exercise of power and control.

Status is not directly related to social class. For example, some people value being recognised as an authority on art or as a person with an outstanding fashion sense. The person is motivated to impress others and be acknowledged as worthy or special rather than 'expert'.

General comments on personality/ability exercises and tests

There are a number of very good and some bad examples of these in use. If you are asked during the recruitment process to do one or more be sure to find out what it is supposed to reveal, and check that you will receive full feedback, i.e. the same results that the recruiter will see. That this is done is a normal condition of using the test.

There are books you can buy which give examples of different kinds of tests, if you want to get some practice. I believe the most important things to do are to read the instructions and the questions carefully and answer truthfully/as well as you can without trying to second guess the test originator.

Whatever the test or exercise it will never reveal more than partial truths about you. Never be afraid to deny something that you know to be wrong or misleading.

A Guide to Job-Hunting on the Internet

The Internet is a revolutionary job-hunting resource. Never before has so much information, advice, expertise and access to job vacancies been available to a person sitting in front of a computer. But this strength is also a weakness: if you are not an expert Internet user the sheer volume of material and resources available can be intimidating. If you're not careful, you could find yourself endlessly checking job-sites and e-mail updates and weeding out heaps of conflicting information, disinformation and irrelevant or out-of-date vacancies.

This appendix is designed to give you a very simple introduction to using the Internet as a job-hunting tool and avoiding common pitfalls. It guides you to some useful websites that can help you get started and lead you to job-sites that are relevant to you. It explains the main things you need to know about a job-site before deciding whether to register with it. Finally, it gives hints on using the Internet for pre-interview research on a potential employer, probably the most important use of all.

Whilst the Internet is constantly growing and much of the information on it changes rapidly, its nature stays the same. What I have tried to do is provide some signposts for the way and a few examples of websites that have a track record.

Before you launch your on-line job search, keep one thing in mind. The Internet doesn't change any of the fundamental rules of job-hunting outlined in this book. It is merely a tool, albeit a very powerful one, that can make your task easier and allow you to cast your net wider than has ever been possible before.

Getting started

If you're the kind of person who likes to get an overview before they launch into a new project you could do worse than check out one of the following sites. Each gives you a panoramic view of Internet job-hunting with lots of reasonable, general advice and dozens of links to other sites, which may be useful. They are US-based, so inevitably have a bias towards US job-sites and towards US job search styles. To the extent that much of their advice is universal they are worth looking at. Be aware however that these are commercial sites with lots to sell (including books!).

Neither carries job ads – they approach the subject as advisers and then point you to job-sites. This may make them more independent in their advice and directions. There are no comparable UK sites.

http://www.rileyguide.com
The Riley Guide is a directory of employment and career information sources and services on the Internet, written by Margaret F. Dikel, probably the foremost expert on Internet job-hunting.

http://www.jobhuntersbible.com
Dick Bolles' on-line companion to his best-selling career guide *What Color is Your Parachute?*

There is also an excellent if slightly different UK-based website:

http://www.careersa-z.co.uk
It is sponsored by Learndirect and apart from links to job sites it provides genuine **information about careers** as well as access to CV writing services, books etc. This means that unlike the US sites, where if you click on Career Advice you will be given a hard sell on how you can quadruple your employment prospects by learning how to write cover letters, instead you are informed about the way to become a Career Advisor! One excellent feature is a brilliant course location service. All you do is fill in your desired subject and your postcode and a

comprehensive list appears. There is also much information about universities and courses.

There are links to specialist job sites and to big general sites. For example, two key words and few clicks of the mouse gets you through to two hundred odd Web Development jobs in London on the Totaljobs site.

Career resources

As you will see once you get going, you can use the Internet at every stage of your job hunt. In addition to the key uses of finding job-sites and researching potential employers (see **The best thing since sliced bread** page 174) you can use the Internet to source employment agencies, CV writing services and do on-line psychometric tests. I do not recommend CV writing services, though there is good general advice available, on *careersa-z.co.uk* for example, as I believe firmly that you should write your own.

Job-sites – what's out there

There are literally tens of thousands of websites around the world that carry job ads. These range from huge sites, such as *monster.com*, operating internationally, across all sectors and all levels of seniority to niche sites catering for a specific sector, geographical location or level of seniority. Most of the large sites are broken down by geography and sector, but rarely offer the depth of industry specific sites. Many job-sites also carry career and job-hunting advice of varying quality and offer additional services like career counselling or CV writing.

Job-sites are owned and operated in different ways. Some are owned by traditional recruitment agencies or headhunters who've added an on-line presence. Others are stand-alone ventures set up purely as Internet job-sites. Yet others belong to media organisations which sensed the threat to the recruitment advertising revenue in their newspapers or magazines and moved their job ads on-line.

As a job seeker you should be aware of who is behind any site before you register your details with them, to make sure they are reliable and reputable. If you don't know who is behind the site, look for the 'about us' and 'contact us' buttons and make the same kind of inquiries you would if dealing with a 'normal' recruitment agency.

Common expressions you may come across are 'in association with' or 'powered by so-and-so'. What this means is that the website you started from has some kind of contractual relationship with 'So and So', with which you are now dealing. For example, on *www.bloomberg.com*, the website of financial information group Bloomberg, you will find that if you click the button offering jobs in the City of London you are led to a jobsearch mechanism 'powered by efinancialcareers'. This means you are dealing with efinancialcareers, via Bloomberg.

Where do the jobs come from?

Job-sites get their vacancies from a variety of sources. Those that belong to a single recruitment agency may get jobs only from that agency. Other sites gather jobs from a wide variety of agencies. Others only take jobs directly from employers and won't let agencies post vacancies. Yet others mix and match. Each of these approaches has its merits. You just need to know what you are dealing with.

How does the site work?

Job-sites are basically about matching employers and candidates. On some sites this is a two-way process in which candidates can search for vacancies and employers or agencies can search for candidates. On other sites, it is one way only. Usually, this means that candidates can search the job ads, but not vice versa. There are some sites that operate purely as candidate databases. Job seekers register their details and wait to be contacted, usually by a recruitment agent or headhunter. (You may wait a long time.)

Once again, each approach has its merits. A two-way process clearly broadens the possibility of a match. It allows employers actively to search you out. On the other hand, although most sites have a mechanism to ensure candidates' identities are not revealed, you may still be nervous about who may have access to your CV or who may find out that you are in the market. Before you register with a job-site, make sure which type it is and how it works.

Registering with a job-site and e-mail alerts

Before you register with a job-site have a good look around it. Assure yourself of all the points raised above. Many sites will also allow you to do a limited search for the kind of jobs you are interested in before you have to register. Do a search and see how many jobs come up, how up to date they are and how relevant they are to you, before deciding whether to register.

You may find that the database throws up hundreds of jobs. If this is the case, 95% of them are probably irrelevant. If the site does not allow you to narrow your search meaningfully, you may not want to proceed especially if registration means that you get automatic e-mail alerts about suitable jobs. Otherwise, you may find your mailbox brimming every day or week with useless e-mails that you need to trawl through in the hope of finding a single gem. E-mail alerts are brilliant if relevant, but a terrible bore if they're not.

Some sites to look at

- ◆ *www.ukjobsguide.co.uk* – Useful first port of call, though confusingly it comes up as *www.uknetguide.co.uk* – A site that leads you to other sites.

- ◆ *www.jobsite.co.uk* – Award-winning job-site with Manpower as a key investor. Carries jobs from recruitment agencies and employers.

- ◆ *www.planetrecruit.com* – A large site that carries recruitment agency jobs and allows candidates to register their CVs and receive appropriate jobs.

- ◆ *www.fish4jobs.com* – Owned by a number of regional newspaper groups and carrying many job ads previously appearing only in newspapers.

- *www.jobserve.com* – Another large, well established site with jobs from recruitment agencies.

- *www.jobtrack.co.uk* – As above.

- *www.totaljobs.com* – As above.

The best thing since sliced bread

You could, if you chose, ignore everything mentioned above and make the perfect career move without ever going near the Internet – except in one respect. The wealth of information now available on-line has raised the standard of expectation among employers about how much a candidate should know about them and their business at a first interview.

Nowadays, if you turn up without having carefully read the company's website and done a basic search on the issues it faces, you will not be seen as a serious candidate. On the other hand, with a little extra effort and know how, you can arrive at the interview impressively prepared.

Where to start researching an employer?

The company's own website
Read all parts of it thoroughly, including bits that may seem irrelevant. For example, sections on graduate recruitment can be enlightening even for an experienced executive because they give an impression of the company's approach to hiring and developing new talent at junior levels.

Look out especially for mission statements, information about the financial state of the company, about key executives, products and services.

Follow any links from the website and do an advanced search on Google (or other comparable search engine) to find other links. This can lead to useful interview questions: 'I see you sponsored the Barcelona conference on Global Custody, is that an area you are particularly targeting?'

Large companies often put their recent announcements and press releases on their website. Read the press releases and then check newspaper and trade press websites to see whether and how the announcements were covered.

Corporate information sites (some of these charge for some information)

◆ *www.hemscott.com* – For information on all UK listed companies and many others. £6 to join for a week – worth considering.

◆ *www.hoovers.com* – A similar, bigger, US-based site with information on listed companies worldwide.

◆ *www.wetfeet.com* – A US-based job seekers website with really good insider guides to many large employers. An excellent website generally.

◆ *www.vault.com* – Similar to the above. Also very good. Charges USD 20–25 for insider guides as does wetfeet.com above.

Industry/professional association websites

These can be very useful for assessing a company's standing within its peer group or identifying individuals from the company who act on an industry-wide level. The person interviewing you may hold a particular office or sit on a committee. Find out via the website and ask a question about it at interview. You will demonstrate that you have done your homework and flatter his/her ego to boot.

Media sites

An extra bonus attaching to many newspaper and specialist or trade websites is an archive search facility that will allow you to find stories by keyword. Although there's a growing trend towards charging for this information, most is available free. Most fee-charging sites also offer free trials. These specialist sites are a first class means of researching a company's main products, suppliers, customers and competitors.

Star story

Ian was a relatively recent client of mine, a fifty-something electrical engineer, specialising in quality management. In 2000 he was made redundant from a company where he had worked for more than 30 years. Since he used the Internet regularly in his working life, it was natural for him to use it in his job search.

Along with traditional job search methods, Ian registered with a number of job-sites, including *planetrecruit.com*, *jobsite.co.uk* and *jobserve.com*. He got sent some junk and a few near misses. The job he eventually got with a printing technology company came through a recruitment agent operating from the other side of the country, who saw Ian's CV on *planetrecruit.com* and contacted him for a vacancy he was trying to fill. Interestingly a local recruitment agent near where Ian lives, who had met Ian and had him on his books, knew about the same job, but had not thought Ian suitable – a fact he has been kicking himself about ever since, says Ian.

Ian learnt about which job-sites to use by trial and error and by comparing notes with colleagues who were made redundant with him. When registering with a site, he says, you have to stipulate what you're looking for in a conscious way. 'Job-sites all work with key word searches. You can very easily get sent every job under the sun, in which case you need to edit your profile or unsubscribe if you can't get it focused more tightly', he says.

Ian found that dealing with all the e-mail alerts he got was very time consuming. He would get the same jobs through from several sites and found that at least 60% of what he was sent was irrelevant. It was also especially difficult to stop the e-mails coming after he had got a job and two years down the line, he is still sometimes being contacted. 'Even if you unsubscribe, you get people contacting you because they think they can interest you in a better job', he says.

Nonetheless, the activity of checking e-mail alerts did have its benefits. 'The number of jobs that come through on the Internet gives you hope. It gives you something to do and keeps you very busy, which is a psychological advantage during a long job search.'

Of course Ian got his career move not because of the Internet but because he met the requirements of the employer and presented himself well at interview. Well done Ian!

But it is a nice story because the Internet, not a meeting, was the means whereby the recruiter demonstrated **his** skill in picking out Ian as a likely candidate.

A word of warning

What follows are less my words than those of the two most respected US internet jobsearch experts, Margaret F. Dikel and Dick Bolles, author of the phenomenally successful *What Color is your Parachute?*

First Margaret Dikel, who runs the Riley Guide website, described by Dick as 'everybody's favorite expert on electronic job-hunting.' She says:

> The internet is merely an added dimension to the traditional job search, and it is not an easy dimension to add. Job hunters need to focus less on the search for job listings and more on the idea of using the information accessible on the internet as a tool for researching organizations and finding possibilities.

Dick Bolles is even more forceful in his views, as expressed on the on-line companion to his famous book. He says:

> If all the resume postings and the job listings you search pay off for you, and you get the job you most desire, great! But if it doesn't please don't take it personally.

> If your job hunt on the internet is fruitless ... you are not alone in your digital dismay. Hear about the disappointing web experiences of some actual job hunters.

I won't quote all of them but here is a selection:

Job hunter #1. I have not had any positive reaction to any of my listings of my resume online. The one exception was a headhunter who asked for my resume. You will get a lot of offers from strange companies or people looking for (sic) things that I would describe as pyramid schemes.

Job hunter #2. It was a waste of my time ... not a single reply!

Job hunter #3. I haven't gotten any responses online. My impression is that if you're not in the computer field, you can pretty much forget finding work online.

I don't agree with the last quoted, or at least not with respect to the UK. The best sites do have jobs of all kinds, though it seems that a higher proportion of IT jobs appear on the internet and often **only** on the internet.

Time

It is easy to waste time surfing the net. As my 'star' Ian says above, checking e-mail alerts keeps you busy, which can be psychologically soothing. It may be better however to limit your internet activity in favour of networking.

In summary

The existence of the Internet ought to have revolutionised careers and job search. In fact it hasn't. The Internet has opened up a huge and useful alternative database both for advertised jobs and company and industry information, which is cheap, available and, usually, up to date. It is above all a wonderful research tool.

Career planning

It also provides a number of job- and career-related sites, where you can explore your psychometric profile, though rarely free of charge, get help with your CV or register it on a site, which **may** be visited by a recruiter.

Network meetings and interviews

You **must** use it when researching companies and organisations with which you have formal job interviews arranged. They will expect you to have done so, and you may need the information to help gauge your interest and suggest areas for discussion. You may also have time to look up sites relevant to network meetings, again because the information you glean may help you better to focus your meeting questions.

Direct approaches

It is useful for tracking down groups of companies you might want to write to, and will enable you to get names of senior people with, we hope, their correct titles, and maybe a brief, if inevitably glowing, character sketch.

Recruitment agencies

Virtually all agencies now place their advertisements for jobs on their websites. So do an increasing number of companies recruiting direct. IT companies were among the first to do this and often do not advertise elsewhere. However the Internet has not yet supplanted the press or trade journals which remain the preferred media for general job advertising. For some time to come you will need to scour all the media.

You can register with many specialist agencies over the net and from many you will receive details of potential jobs. Try your luck!

Finally

There is nothing magic about the Internet. It is another fast and convenient method of transmitting and accessing data, nothing else. All the usual rules of job search apply.

Career Planning Exercises

If you know exactly what you want for your next career move this appendix may be of little interest. But if you want to cross-check your views or explore other options, or especially if you are uncertain about your career plans the exercises in this appendix may be of value.

They are only valid if you accept the premise that the better you know yourself the more likely you are to be able to determine what sort of work will best satisfy your needs and wants. Knowing what drives you in career terms (see Career Drivers in Appendix II) and what your preferences, in terms of judging and perceiving, are (see MBTI® in Appendix II) will certainly help, and there are many other psychometric exercises you can do.

The suggestions that follow are not new. They have been around for many years and are based on the assumption that whatever we **do and enjoy,** and which could earn us money, is **potentially** what would give us satisfaction as the basis of a career. Potentially because many enjoyable activities are best pursued as hobbies, interests or pastimes.

The trouble is that we do not see ourselves as others do. This means that any investigations we try to conduct need to be in some way indirect. So here are a few.

Job advertisements – a little light reading

◆ Try one of the non-specialist sections and pick a dozen or so advertisements at random.

♦ Do not consider whether the job is one you could do or even whether it interests you.

♦ Take a highlighter and mark any phrases or isolated words that appeal to you. These may come from the job or person description or from the advertising puff about the organisation.

♦ Do it quite quickly without dwelling long on anything and mark only definite likes, but don't worry if you find you are picking out the same things several times over.

♦ Now look at what you have marked. Write the passages on small Post-it notes and arrange them in groups, which in some way go together.

♦ What does it say to you? What does it say to a good friend or to your partner?

♦ Try it again a week later.

It is important not to analyse to death an exercise like this. It may tell you nothing you did not know already. On the other hand it may give you an important insight into one thing. That you really **need** to do something creative, or that a **big company** culture is something you crave.

Open advice from a friend

This is a simple exercise you can do, which has its uses in CV preparation too (see Appendix I).

Ask your partner or a good friend or friends, or anyone who knows you well and whose opinion you respect to jot down what they consider to be:

a) your strengths
b) areas needing a little attention

c) what would make you happy in your career.

It is extremely important that they each do this as honestly as they know how and that they use these headings rather than some similar ones they have made up. Perhaps the best way is for them to imagine themselves writing this in confidence to a professional career adviser at his/her request, and to whom you have paid an enormous sum of money to help you.

If they ask how much to write or what kind of topics they should address, give them no help at all. You want their perception unsullied and free of influence from you. You may be surprised at the kind of responses you get. Be sure to thank them even if you don't agree with everything they write.

Mary Special

Strengths

Mary is really good at finding another way of looking at things. I think it's because she never seems to be in a hurry, but takes time to listen and asks questions which I hadn't thought of. I value her counsel always.

She has a good sense of humour mostly (see below) and a happy disposition. She is suspiciously good at crosswords.

She is a good organiser of other people, parties, events, etc, and is very good at persuading people to do more than they intended, but they end up enjoying it nevertheless. I think she must be a good picker.

Areas needing a little attention

After a few drinks Mary thinks she is a top-class impressionist (Maggie T, Posh S et al). She **isn't.** She would do well to forget this theatrical tendency. When sober (which is to be fair most of the time – even at a party) she has a tendency to put herself down, only subtly but enough for some people to believe her and therefore underrate her, which is a pity. Or is it a cunning plan?

What would make her happy in her career

This is difficult, but she really ought to do something involving sorting out difficult people problems, or the problems people encounter with systems. She could also do with more responsibility and intellectual challenge. I think she would blossom if given her head.

Clare Luker

It may seem a little unnatural for Clare to write about Mary in the third person and then send it to her, but it should make it easier for her to stand back a little. It remains, however, an intensely personal perception and therein lies its value. By definition Mary knows Clare well and respects her views, she is a radio actress always in work, so perhaps the awful impressions will cease.

Whom to ask for what?

'What' is defined by the headings above, but you will get a slightly different angle from a personal friend than from your partner or from a work colleague. It really doesn't matter who you choose. If you believe you behave entirely differently at work from how you behave with friends or at home, you are either mistaken or know exactly why this is so, and will not ask for input from inappropriate sources.

Autobiography of your working life

This is not for everyone. If your working life has been consistently painful and utterly hateful to you, there is not much point in writing it down in all its misery. But the basic proposal is that you write a history of your working life, in chronological order, concentrating on the detail of the functions that you carried out and also particularly on those parts that gave you the most satisfaction.

It is sometimes suggested that for anyone wishing to change career direction this cannot help. Providing, however, it does not come into the painful/hateful category above it will help you to chart your development over time and to recall small items of importance as well as people you worked for and with, who have influenced you one way or another.

Our past is ourselves in the sense that we have spent all our lives ascribing meaning to, or trying to make sense of, each and every one of our experiences. We all construct our own view of the world using our senses and our brain. In turn the interpretations we make influence how we think, feel and act. We become to a considerable extent the products of our own meaning structure. What we are going to do, in terms of paid work, needs to be related to who we are **now,** products of our past.

For a fuller discussion of 'meaning structure' and other wonders read Dorothy Rowe's *Guide to Life* (HarperCollins, 1995).

The interest in writing an autobiography of your working life lies in the fact that you will be interpreting your most distant past, not as you did at the time it was your immediate past, but now as you are today. Much of it will look different, and some core elements might register as important for you in your future career.

If this exercise seems rather airy-fairy to you just ignore it. It certainly works best when your career to date has been enjoyable and fulfilling.

Exercises for fun – and sometimes revelation

◆ **Write your own obituary.**

Sadly you just died, sometime last week, nevertheless you have the opportunity of putting a gloss on your truncated life. Remember that obituaries are always flattering, and this is to be no exception. It is going to appear in *The Times,* and all your relatives, friends and acquaintances are waiting impatiently to read about all the aspects of you that they did not know, as well as to relive the memory of those they were familiar with. Do not let them down. They want to remember you with respect and affection in their hearts. They also want to know what else you would have achieved, had your life not been so cruelly cut short.

♦ **Baby for sale.**

Write an advertisement for yourself as a newly born baby. As a rough guide to style and length think about how such an advertisement might appear if placed on a postcard in a local newsagent's shop. For the sake of the exercise you may assume that most of your character, attitudes and abilities are built in already. The baby is willing to acquire learning and skills and you may even have some ideas about what and which. You will also probably like to specify the kind of household, siblings or absence of, parent(s) to which the baby in question is most likely to appeal. This baby wants to be sold into an ideal environment, ideal that is from your point of view.

Put these exercises away somewhere and look them out a couple of weeks later and ask yourself the following questions:

♦ What, if anything, do these two exercises say about you?

♦ What is important and what is missing?

♦ What can you add to your label or to your focus?

♦ What is stopping you being anything you want to be?

Bibliography

Bridges, William (1995), *Jobshift*. London: Nicholas Brealey Publishing Ltd.

Briggs, Isabel Myers with Peter B. Myers (1995), *Gifts Differing*. Palo Alto, CA: Davies-Black Publishing.

Eggert, Max (1992), *The Perfect CV*. London: Century Business.

Leeds, Dorothy (1993), *Secrets of Successful Interviews*. London: Judy Piatkus (Publishers) Ltd.

Rowe, Dorothy (1995), *Guide to Life*. London: HarperCollinsPublishers.

Schein, E.H. (1990), *Career Anchors*. San Diego, CA: Pfeiffer & Company.

Useful Addresses

Chartered Institute of Marketing
Moor Hall
Cookham
Maidenhead
Berks SL6 9QH
Tel: 01628 427 120

Executive Grapevine International Limited
New Barnes Mill
Cottonmill Lane
St. Albans AL1 2HA
Tel: 01727 844 335
e-mail: executive.grapevine@dial.pipex.com
www.d-net.com/executive.grapevine

Federation of Recruitment & Employment Services (FRES)
36–38 Mortimer Street
London W1N 7RB
Tel: 020 7323 4300

Institute of Chartered Accountants in England & Wales (ICAEW)
PO Box 433
Chartered Accountants Hall
Moorgate Place
London EC2P 2BJ
Tel: 020 7920 8100

Institute of Chartered Accountants in Scotland
27 Queen Street
Edinburgh EH2 1LA
Tel: 01312 225 673

Green Associates
Hilltop Cottage
Lees Hill
South Warnborough
Hook
Hants RG29 1RQ
Tel: 01256 862742
e-mail: grahamgreen@counselling100.freeserve.co.uk

Jo Ouston & Co
Lower Ground Floor
Nelson House
Dolphin Square
London SW1V 3NY
Tel: 020 7821 8299
e-mail: info@joouston.co.uk
www.joouston.co.uk

The Law Society
Law Society's Hall
113 Chancery Lane
London WC2A 1PL
Tel: 020 7242 1222

Index